REST IN CHRIST

REST IN CHRIST

Gerald A. Klingbeil
Chantal J. Klingbeil

Pacific Press®
Publishing Association
Nampa, Idaho | www.pacificpress.com

Cover design and illustration by Lars Justinen

The authors assume full responsibility for the accuracy of all facts and quotations as cited in this book.

Additional copies of this book are available for purchase by calling toll-free 1-800-765-6955 or by visiting https://AdventistBookCenter.com.

Library of Congress Cataloging-in-Publication Data

Names: Klingbeil, Gerald A., 1964- author. | Klingbeil, Chantal J., 1970- author.
Title: Rest in Christ / Gerald and Chantal Klingbeil.
Description: Nampa, Idaho : Pacific Press Publishing Association, [2021] | Includes bibliographical references. | Summary: "Rest in Christ reviews the principles of finding rest in Jesus Christ. It shows how sitting at the feet of Jesus can bring genuine spiritual, mental, relational, and physical rest"— Provided by publisher.
Identifiers: LCCN 2020048195 (print) | LCCN 2020048196 (ebook) | ISBN 9780816367054 | ISBN 9780816367061 (ebook)
Subjects: LCSH: Rest—Religious aspects—Christianity. | General Conference of Seventh-Day Adventists—Doctrines.
Classification: LCC BV4597.55 .K554 2021 (print) | LCC BV4597.55 (ebook) | DDC 248.4/86732—dc23
LC record available at https://lccn.loc.gov/2020048195
LC ebook record available at https://lccn.loc.gov/2020048196

June 2021

Dedication

To our parents—Esmé and Robert Ross, and Marianne and Armin Klingbeil—who, from early on, modeled confidence and trust in the God who offers true rest in Him.

Contents

Preface

This book is about rest. Rest has become a hot commodity in our restless age. Managers and CEOs pay hefty sums to participate in workshops and seminars on ways to really find rest. Therapists and counselors diagnose an increasing sense of restlessness and disconnectedness—from ourselves and from the people around us.

This is *not* a self-help book, offering ten easy steps to find rest. Based on our reading of Scripture, we have gone a different route. We follow closely the invitation of the Man from Galilee to "come"—especially those who feel "weary and burdened"—and experience His kind of rest (Matthew 11:28). This rest is costly, for it requires us to surrender our own ways of creating rest. This rest is also countercultural, for it involves sitting at the feet of the Master while life rushes by all around us.

In our journey to find this rest, we noticed that the biblical idea of rest touches on many key concepts of biblical faith. These include health, sin, salvation, surrender, forgiveness, death and dying, the Sabbath, the way we interpret Scripture, the second coming of Jesus, and our sense of mission.

While this book keeps pace with the flow of our thoughts found in the *Adult Sabbath School Bible Study Guide*, we consciously tried to avoid repeating the concepts and texts discussed there. We did this in order to create a book that could stand on its own and also be shared with others who are on a journey to find this rest.

Each chapter is divided into six sections. Following a brief introduction to the chapter's topic, we look at issues related to the topic and questions of worldview, as the power of the underlying worldview is often overlooked when these subjects are addressed. "Digging deep," the central section of the chapter, seeks to focus more profoundly on key biblical texts or sections related to the topic of the chapter. The next section, "Implications," applies the key ideas discovered in the earlier sections to practical living. Finally, we conclude each chapter with an invitation to "take a breather." This section usually contains several Bible promises or challenges, followed by a short reflection.

As a couple, we have spent the last five years thinking, preaching, and writing about this important topic. The process was not always restful, but both of us have felt blessed by the God who invited His creation to rest at the end of a busy Creation week to enjoy intimacy and communion. We pray that reading this book will draw you closer to the Source of all rest and encourage you to rest in His grace.

One

Restless 24-7

John's schedule was always full, yet you could always depend on him to squeeze in one more appointment. He was a well-liked, hard-working department director who was married to a beautiful woman. As a father of two young boys, John never had a dull moment. Soccer practice, fishing trips with his sons, dinners at the golf club, and yachting with his wife on weekends kept him busy. Yet no one could have known that John had to keep the busyness going. If he stopped for even a moment, the dull ache of loneliness would threaten to drown out any meaning in his life.

Issue—when busyness cannot save us from loneliness
We live in a world that is constantly in the "on" mode. We are busy 24-7. Our jobs demand continual engagement. Our families need attention. Add to that a good dose of social media and the ever-demanding rhythms of living in our connected world, and we eventually find ourselves physically and emotionally exhausted.

One would imagine that the increased availability of digital connections and our ability to travel easily would help us to find community and balance. Unlike our grandparents, who often grew up in small communities or long-established neighborhoods where everyone knew everyone, we often feel lonely and—in spite of our many digital connections—disconnected. Busyness is not an antidote for loneliness.

Research has shown that loneliness affects a growing swath of people. In the United Kingdom, nearly 20 percent of the population say they are always or often lonely.[1] In the United States, between 25 and 60 percent of older Americans are lonely, especially Americans fifty and over.[2] Loneliness, however, affects many beyond the older population groups. According to a Viceland UK census, loneliness is the number one fear of young people today—ranking ahead of losing a home or a job.[3]

Loneliness can be destructive, devastating, and even deadly—especially when it is not immediately visible. Who could have known that John, who was constantly busy at work and at home, really felt disconnected and lonely and tried to use his busyness as a means of overcoming the ultimate sense of being alone?

Loneliness is not linked to a particular personality trait, like being an introvert or an extrovert. Introverts and extroverts (and any other personality types) may relate differently to loneliness, yet we are all touched negatively by the experience of loneliness.

The impact of loneliness on our health is staggering. Being lonely has a health risk factor equivalent to smoking fifteen cigarettes per day, shortening one's life span by eight years.[4] The mortality rate of lonely people increases significantly, in line with other high risk factors, such as cancer and neurodegenerative diseases.[5] Preliminary research also suggests a close link between loneliness and cardiovascular problems.[6] While living in a 24-7 world, connected by media and ever-expanding social networks, should, theoretically, offer more community, the fact is that loneliness is a key factor affecting the health and well-being of Western societies.

Worldview—created for community

Against this backdrop of modern loneliness, one wonders whether the ancients faced a similar challenge. People living in the world of the Bible were part of a community-dense culture and context.[7] Dutch sociologist Geert Hofstede described four relevant dimensions of cultures; one of them directly affects the issue of restlessness and loneliness.[8] Individualism versus collectivism seems to focus, at least at first glance, on the density of one's social networks. People living in Manila or Accra look at the world through the lens of *we* instead of *I*. Persons living in Berlin, Budapest, or Boston, on the other hand, experience themselves first and foremost as individuals and focus less on the larger community.

A close reading of the Bible clearly underlines the concept of the collective nature of culture and society in the biblical world. Abraham was not called out of Ur alone but was part of a larger family and clan, which included numerous male servants (Genesis 14:14)—and many more women and children. God's covenant with him, visualized in the covenant sign of circumcision (Genesis 17:10–14), was applied to all male members of his household (verses 23–27), and there is no indication of individual consultation. Good kings inspired their people to a closer walk with God. In contrast, the leadership of evil kings often resulted in idolatry and the rupture of Israel's covenant with the Lord. (A good example of this can be found in 2 Chronicles 14:2–5.)

The Ten Commandments suggest that sin directly affects larger communities and entire generations—up to the fourth generation (Exodus 20:5; 34:7; Deuteronomy 5:9). At the same time, the Bible is also clear that there is no collective guilt (Deuteronomy 24:16). The fact that people in the ancient world lived in three- to four-generation families may explain the language of the Ten Commandments and the direct effects of sin on several generations.[9] *We* was undoubtedly more important than *I* in biblical times, yet an even stronger emphasis on community did not result in less loneliness.

Digging deep—sin separates us from God and one another
The Creation story in Genesis 1 and 2 unmistakably emphasizes that

we were made for community—beginning with a nuclear family but also involving the networks of larger family structures, including clan and tribes. Sin, however, not only introduced doubt and distrust, ultimately resulting in rebellion, but also separated us from God and those we love and need the most.

Genesis 3:1 suggests that Eve must have wandered away from Adam as she explores their garden home. Somehow, she feels drawn to the one tree that God had set apart. Its intriguing name—"the tree of the knowledge of good and evil" (Genesis 2:17)—is reason enough to have a closer look. Imagine her surprise when she suddenly sees a strikingly beautiful serpent that can speak. The serpent's question, "Has God indeed said, 'You shall not eat of every tree of the garden'?" (Genesis 3:1, NKJV), does not represent a frontal attack against the divine order. Instead, it sows doubt and distrust in Eve's mind. Then and now, the main battlefield is the human mind and our perception of God's character. Eve does not skip a beat and enters into a conversation with the serpent adversary (verses 2–5). The serpent's bold contradiction of the divine command, "You will not surely die" (verse 4, NKJV), is followed by a dark insinuation of ulterior divine motives: "For God knows that in the day you eat of it [the fruit] your eyes will be opened, and you will be like God, knowing good and evil" (verse 5, NKJV). Knowledge is an alluring currency, and it works in Eve's case. She eats from the forbidden fruit. Her next reported action is sharing the fruit with Adam (verse 6). This is the first time Adam appears in this narrative. Between the terse lines of Genesis 3, we can imagine the struggle that Adam experiences, torn between faithfulness to God's commandment and his commitment to his life partner. Ellen White describes this pivotal moment poignantly: "Adam understood that his companion had transgressed the command of God, disregarded the only prohibition laid upon them as a test of their fidelity and love. There was a terrible struggle in his mind."[10]

We still experience the consequences of Eve's and Adam's choices. Sin has separated us from God—and also from one another.

Selfishness, greed, abuse, and so many more destructive negatives have resulted from this one decision that changed who we were. Instead of reflecting God's image and likeness, we have become self-centered and hurtful and abusive, even if we manage to cloak ourselves behind a façade of civility. While there are many causes of loneliness, sin's separation of God's creation is definitely among the top five.

God's search for His creation, however, offers hope in a sad story. His "Where are you?" (verse 9) continues to echo down the ages and reaches us in unexpected places. In one of His most famous parables, Jesus tells of a son who demanded his inheritance from his father, and after receiving it, he left home and managed to waste everything (Luke 15:11–32). He finds himself eking out an existence as a swineherd, which was an unimaginable occupation for any Jewish son. Finally, he comes to his senses and decides to return home and throw himself at his father's mercy. As he walks the familiar road leading to his father's house, he is surprised to see his father running full throttle toward him to embrace him and kiss him. He is home and loved and forgiven, for God always takes the first step to draw His wayward children back to Him (John 6:44). Beginning in Eden, God has always been searching for His fallen creation and continues to search for the lost and lonely.

Implications—combating restlessness and loneliness
Here are some practical, hands-on tips for combating loneliness:

1. *Recognize our restlessness and loneliness*, and acknowledge that we need outside help. Restlessness and loneliness are as real conditions as being hungry or thirsty.
2. *Consciously form connections.* Before we can form meaningful connections with the people around us, however, we need to learn to connect with ourselves. Part of that process involves the recognition that we are loved and cherished, even with our imperfections and challenges. God's yes to us in Jesus Christ is foundational for this realization.

3. *Form meaningful connections with others* as the first step in breaking negative thought patterns and cognitive routes. Patterns are
   not easily changed, for they have become our default modes of
   operation. Sometimes we may need to find professional help to
   break destructive patterns.
4. *Serve others in the community.* Serving others is a wonderful way
   to overcome loneliness and uncertainty as we realize that we are
   an intricate part of something bigger than ourselves. Studies
   suggest that volunteering for a cause and working with others for
   a greater good are effective therapies for loneliness and help us to
   be better braced against the uncertainties of life.[11]

Take a breather—trust His promises
The Bible is full of divine promises offering hope to those who experience restlessness, loneliness, and darkness. Here are five examples.

*"Be strong and courageous. Do not be afraid or terrified because of
them, for the* LORD *your God goes with you; he will never leave you nor
forsake you" (Deuteronomy 31:6).* These words are directed to people
living on the threshold of change. Moses is about to die, and a new
leader, Joshua, has been appointed. God promises His people and the
future leader that He will never leave them or forsake them. Intriguingly, in Hebrew, the point of reference—"you"—in this sentence
refers to an individual. God's promise is personal.

> *Even though I walk*
> *through the darkest valley,*
> *I will fear no evil,*
> *for you are with me;*
> *your rod and your staff,*
> *they comfort me (Psalm 23:4).*

This text sits right in the center of one of the most loved and best-known
psalms of the Hebrew Bible. It is a comforting picture to imagine the

Good Shepherd walking with us through the dark moments. In the midst of uncertainty, danger, and restlessness, we can rest in Him, for He promises to be with us and protect us in the midst of our challenges and fears.

"Come near to God and he will come near to you" (James 4:8). When children are afraid, they instinctively draw close to the person they trust and love. Proximity means safety and assurance. While the actual danger may not have disappeared, just knowing that Papa or Mama is close by makes the child relax. The New Testament tells us that God moves very close to us. In fact, His incarnation is the best illustration of this principle. The Bible says that Jesus came to carry our pain and suffer our punishment, and He did not use the VIP lounge or palace as His earthly headquarters. People came close to Him: the discouraged, the sick, the abused, the restless, and the weary. They all came to experience love, grace, and transformation. Drawing close to God changes us and brings us closer to each other.

"Come to me, all you who are weary and burdened, and I will give you rest" (Matthew 11:28). When Jesus makes this powerful statement, He seems to think of a community of believers because the Greek personal pronoun used here is plural. Rest is not only extended to a group of insiders or those with special privileges—rest and recovery from burdens and uncertainty are offered to *all* who come.

"So in Christ we, though many, form one body, and each member belongs to all the others" (Romans 12:5). Paul's letter to the church in Rome is a message to people dealing with the constant threat of persecution and death. Uncertainty was a way of life for them. They were also part of a church where Jews and Gentiles were learning how to build bridges to one another. The body imagery used by Paul highlights our need for connectedness. We all like to belong and feel needed.

But beyond connectedness, Paul's words also point to shared service. Each member of the body has been gifted to serve together purposefully and become a blessing to others. Serving others in community is a wonderful way to overcome loneliness and uncertainty.

1. See the relevant data, based on research from 2016, at "Loneliness Research," Campaign to End Loneliness, accessed March 5, 2020, https://www.campaigntoendloneliness.org/loneliness-research/.

2. Charlotte S. Yeh, "The Power and Prevalence of Loneliness," *Harvard Health Blog*, January 13, 2017, https://www.health.harvard.edu/blog/the-power-and-prevalence-of-loneliness-2017011310977.

3. See Hannah Ewens, "What Young People Fear the Most," *Vice*, September 21, 2016, https://www.vice.com/en_uk/article/nnyk37/what-vice-readers-fear-the-most-hannah-ewens-love-loneliness.

4. Yeh, "Power and Prevalence"; "The Facts on Loneliness," Campaign to End Loneliness, accessed March 5, 2020, https://www.campaigntoendloneliness.org/the-facts-on-loneliness/.

5. Julianne Holt-Lunstad, Timothy B. Smith, and J. Bradley Layton, "Social Relationships and Mortality Risk: A Meta-analytic Review," *PLOS Medicine* 7, no. 7 (July 27, 2010): https://doi.org/10.1371/journal.pmed.1000316.

6. Ning Xia and Huige Li, "Loneliness, Social Isolation, and Cardiovascular Health," *Antioxidants & Redox Signaling* 28, no. 9 (2018): 837–851, https://www.ncbi.nlm.nih.gov/pmc/articles/PMC5831910/.

7. See the discussion in Gerald A. Klingbeil, "Between 'I' and 'We': The Anthropology of the Hebrew Bible and Its Importance for a 21st-Century Ecclesiology," *Bulletin for Biblical Research* 19, no. 3 (2009): 319–339.

8. Geert Hofstede, *Cultures and Organizations: Software of the Mind*, rev. ed. (New York: McGraw Hill, 1997), 3–138. The other dimensions discussed by Hofstede include (1) power versus lack of power, (2) feminine versus masculine, and (3) certainty versus uncertainty.

9. Research studying the propensity of children or grandchildren of alcoholics toward alcohol addiction underlines this notion of one's actions affecting more than the individual.

10. Ellen G. White, *Patriarchs and Prophets* (Mountain View, CA: Pacific Press®, 1958), 56.

11. Tchiki Davis, "Feeling Lonely? Discover 18 Ways to Overcome Loneliness," *Click Here for Happiness* (blog), *Psychology Today*, February 18, 2019, https://www.psychologytoday.com/us/blog/click-here-happiness/201902/feeling-lonely-discover-18-ways-overcome-loneliness.

- Amnesia — ingratitude
. Megalomania — insubordination
. Phobia — insecurity. (grasshopper Syndrome)
3. Delusional Schizophrenia — Insanity.

Restless and Rebellious

Ai Fen was a Chinese medical doctor and director of the emergency department of the Central Hospital of Wuhan. On December 18, 2019, she examined a patient who worked at the Huanan Seafood Wholesale Market and had a bad pulmonary infection. On December 27, she received a second patient with a similar pulmonary infection. She was the first to suspect that a new coronavirus was in circulation. Within months, countries all over the world were in lockdowns with soaring death tolls and shaken economies, as the new coronavirus, named COVID-19, quickly spread.[1]

There are many things that cannot be seen with the naked eye that are both highly contagious and deadly if not recognized and dealt with quickly. Restlessness is one of these things. It spreads swiftly from person to person and can soon turn into open rebellion with deadly results. Restlessness can go viral rapidly, and it affects not only individuals but entire communities.

Issue—the power of speech
As human beings, we were created with the ability to communicate intelligently through language. This ability for meaningful and abstract

speech is part and parcel of having been created in the image and likeness of the God who created by simply speaking (Genesis 1:26–28; John
1:1–3, 14). While we cannot create by our words to the extent that God
can, there are things less tangible but no less real that we can create.
Interestingly, the abuse of language led to the dispersion and scattering
of humanity and the development of distinct languages (Genesis 11),
ultimately curtailing the human ability to communicate freely. We can
encourage and help with our words, but we can also cause tremendous
pain, damage others, and destroy faith with our words.

Everything we say "exerts an influence" and sets in motion an action
that always involves others. In reality, what I say is not just my business
because each of us is "a part of the great web of humanity"; we are
interlinked through "our individual threads of influence."[2] Jesus used
His words to inspire faith and draw others to God. As His followers,
we will want to be sensitive to the Holy Spirit's promptings and allow
Him to lead us to use this creative power in the most positive way.

There is an intimate connection between who we really are and what
we speak about. When we have a full glass of water and bump the
glass, water will come out—not orange juice or lemonade. Whatever
we are on the inside will ultimately come to the outside. We will
overflow with what we really are.

Our words are more than an indication of our character and who
we really are. We influence others by our language and words and also
influence ourselves. Sometimes, in a spur-of-the-moment reaction, we
may say something that we don't really believe or may deliberately lie.
But expression often deepens impression, and we affect others and
ourselves when we hear ourselves repeat these statements. Having once
expressed an opinion or a decision, we are often too proud to retract
it and instead try to prove ourselves right. We come to believe our own
lies about God, ourselves, or others. This self-made prison is the most
difficult to escape.

Worldview—restlessness in heaven

The great cosmic battle between good and evil rages all around us and often within us. It began with a rebellion in heaven, but before that, there was restlessness.

How could there be restlessness in heaven? we wonder. *Heaven is a perfect place.* It is the very place where the God who is love (see 1 John 4:8) resides—the place where everyone existed in perfect harmony and reflected unselfish love. It is the place where there had never been a note of discord. And right there, restlessness began with one of the most honored and powerful inhabitants of heaven. Lucifer, who was known as the son of the morning, one of the covering cherubs who lived in God's immediate presence, began to change (Isaiah 14). Little by little, inconspicuously at first, something started stirring, and a nameless restlessness began brewing—a quiet longing for change and redirection.

All created beings directed their affections and allegiance to God, but Lucifer began to long for this affection to be redirected to him. Once this restlessness had matured into pride and taken firm root in him, he went out from God's presence to diffuse a spirit of restlessness among the angels under the guise of a call to freedom. Quietly, he set the rumor mill in operation, misconstruing and distorting God's words and actions to make them appear in a strange new light and cause dissatisfaction. Quietly and secretly, this fermenting restlessness grew into an open rebellion that shattered heaven's bliss and went on to have a cosmic fallout that affected every created being in the universe and did not even leave God Himself unscarred. Incredibly, all of this woe and misery began with restlessness.

Digging deep—the anatomy of rebellion

The book of Numbers has a unique structure, pivoting around two generations of Israel—old and new.[3] A quick scan of the first ten chapters of Numbers results in many references to faithful compliance: God tells Moses (and, by extension, Israel) to count all the men aged twenty and above—*check* (Numbers 1:54). God organizes Israel's living space and the camp arrangements—*check* (Numbers 2:34). When God orders a census of the Levites, Moses and the people comply (Numbers 3:16). The firstborns are to be numbered and redeemed—*check* (verse 42). When the Levites need to be formally ordained for their special ministry, Moses and the people follow through (Numbers 8:20). In every instance, there is a fulfillment formula that sounds something like this: "And X did Y according to the word of the Lord." God speaks, and Moses and the people comply.

Right at the end of Numbers 10, Israel departs from Mount Sinai, en route to the Promised Land. Old Testament scholar Dennis Cole comments poignantly: "Just when things look the brightest and most promising, with the Lord leading the people by the cloud of his presence in a glorious march from the mountain where they have encountered him toward a Promised Land of abundance and freedom, the story takes a dramatic turn."[4] Beginning in Numbers 11, the façade begins to crack. Instead of obedience (or at least compliance), we find complaints, suspicion, and even open rebellion. Everyone is affected. It starts with a mixed multitude and catches on with the people, even affecting Moses as he complains to God about his lot of leading a wayward people. Miriam and Aaron weigh in and criticize not only Moses' leadership but also his marriage and tribal loyalty. When the going gets tough, when the time gets longer, erstwhile obedient Israel suddenly becomes suspicious, complaining, and double-guessing Israel.

An example of the anatomy of the murmurings can be found in Numbers 12. The chapter follows a veritable collection of complaints described in Numbers 11. It seems that the murmurings tend to multiply because the spirit behind them is contagious. The year 2020 illustrates how quickly one can catch a contagious virus. The arrival of COVID-19 and the attempts of governments around the world to contain the pandemic are helpful reminders of the reality of contagion in our world. Sin and rebellion, however, are even more contagious than COVID-19.

The first two verses of Numbers 12 teach a significant lesson: *the purported reason for a complaint may not always be its true cause.* Verse 1 tells us that Miriam and Aaron talk "against Moses because of his Cushite wife." Twice, the ethnic origin of Zipporah is mentioned, which is another way of pushing their noses into a problem: Moses has married a Cushite—a foreigner and an outsider. *Imagine that!* While Moses' marriage (and questions of influence) may have been an issue, the real complaint goes much deeper: "God does not only speak through Moses—He has also spoken through us" (see verse 2). The core issue of Aaron and Miriam's murmurings does not involve some abstract theological point of contention concerning revelation. Miriam and Aaron feel cut out; they want to belong to the inside circle. Verse 2 closes with the ominous "And the LORD heard it" (NKJV), reminding us that *there is a heavenly dimension to our complaints and murmurings,* especially when they happen inside the church.

God's response to this complaint is quick and decisive. After Aaron, Miriam, and Moses gather at the entrance of the tabernacle, the Lord comes down in a pillar of cloud. This is a crucial moment, affecting divine leadership and communication, thus God's swift response. It seems as if Aaron and Miriam have not been part of the seventy elders that God had empowered to share Moses' leadership duties, as detailed in Numbers 11:16–25. Perhaps they are jealous of Moses' privileged standing with God. Perhaps they have gotten used to being the "top dogs" and now feel unappreciated. The Bible is not entirely clear as to the true reason for their murmurings. Scripture, however, is unequivocally clear about God's response. "Why then were you not afraid to speak against My servant Moses?" (Numbers 12:8, NKJV).

Here is another valuable lesson from Numbers 12: *When we murmur and mumble against other people (or God), we forget who we really are and our position in life.* We are not the center of the universe. We are frail human beings with large egos, often lacking sound judgment and true recognition of our place in life.

Implications—presumption and faith

Of all the counterfeits that Satan has managed to bring into religion, presumption is perhaps one of the most difficult to sense because it lies close to real faith. After Israel refuses to go into the land of Canaan to conquer the land that God has promised them, the Israelites give us a vivid example of just how presumption works. Things reach a fever pitch with the ten spies' negative reports, and people are so worked up that they are about to stone their leaders and the two spies who try to talk faith. That's the moment when God steps in. He spells out the consequences for their behavior: they will go back to the desert for forty years, and only their children will inherit the land. Upon hearing this declaration, the Israelites quickly swing from doubt and lack of faith to presumption. "We have sinned," they say. "We will go up to the place the Lord promised" (see Numbers 14:40).

Their half-hearted commitment is like a poorly administered vaccination; it doesn't work. Today, doctors recommend a hepatitis B vaccination right after birth, within the first twenty-four hours of life. That's a good beginning. But if there are not two or three booster vaccinations following that—administered at the right time and in the right doses—there is no protection against hepatitis B whatsoever.

Israel's stubborn turnaround, reported in the last verses of Numbers 14, results in death and disappointment for them. They refuse to accept God's new directions and stubbornly launch an attack without the ark of the covenant or Moses' leadership.

Presumption is costly. It leads to death and is often powered by fear. Because we are afraid of something, we make decisions we later regret. Fear led Israel to reject God's original plan—particularly considering the giants of the land. Rejecting God's plan then led them to rebel. Fear of divine retribution ultimately made them act presumptuously, and the vicious circle was completed.

Take a breather—good counsel

Biblical proverbs are a treasure trove of good counsel, even though they make us feel uncomfortable sometimes, for they are direct and to the point. The book of Proverbs deals with the practice of living in the real world. Wisdom in Scripture is not an intellectual exercise or a complex philosophical equation. Wisdom, according to Old Testament scholar Roy B. Zuck, "means being skillful and successful in one's relationships and responsibilities. It involves observing and following the Creator's principles of order in the moral universe."[5] Proverbs 9:10 highlights this close link between recognizing the Creator's principles of order and our moral choices: "The fear of the LORD is the beginning of wisdom, and knowledge of the Holy One is understanding."

Here are three texts offering us good counsel as we navigate a world that is characterized by restlessness and rebellion.

"*The words of the reckless pierce like swords, but the tongue of the wise brings healing*" *(Proverbs 12:18).* We do not have to live on Twitter or other social media platforms to recognize the inflammatory nature of careless words. The wrong word in a crucial moment can be like pouring gasoline on a smoldering fire. God, however, invites us to be different. Instead of bringing hurt by our words or, using the imagery found in the biblical text, slashing wildly with a sword, the followers of the Man of Galilee are to bring healing through their words. Intriguingly, the Hebrew word referencing reckless speech is also used to describe the declaration that burst from Moses' lips at the waters of Meribah (Psalm 106:32, 33; cf. Numbers 20:8–12), which ultimately kept him from entering the Promised Land.[6]

"*A gentle answer turns away wrath, but a harsh word stirs up anger*" *(Proverbs 15:1).* Contemporary culture often mistakes gentleness with weakness. As followers of Jesus, we are invited to respond compassionately and gently. This is not an invitation to avoid conflict or downplay truth. Rather, it reminds us that our speech is powerful and is able to transform critical moments. Jesus blesses those who have the ability to make peace in words and deeds (Matthew 5:9).

"*Get rid of all bitterness, rage and anger, brawling and slander, along with every form of malice*" *(Ephesians 4:31).* This New Testament example of wise counsel, along with verse 32, represents the apex of this chapter. Paul encourages his readers to walk in unity in verses 1–6, reminds them that they all have been endowed with spiritual gifts to build up the body of Christ in verses 7–16, and then paints the picture of God's new creation, transformed by His Spirit. The final section, where verse 31 is found, includes practical admonitions to "not grieve" God's Spirit (verse 30). Getting rid of "bitterness, rage and anger, brawling and slander," and all types of malice is not something we can do (verse 31). The Greek verb translated in the New International Version as "get rid of" is really a passive form, suggesting that God does the removing. We have to face the basic truth that only God can remove characteristics that diminish the new creation that He is committed to transforming us into.

Fortunately, Paul doesn't conclude this chapter with verse 31. He recognizes that we cannot stop at removing evil. Instead, we are invited to allow God's Spirit to plant new qualities into our character: "And be kind to one another, tenderhearted, forgiving one another, even as God in Christ forgave you" (verse 32, NKJV).

1. Lily Kuo, "Coronavirus: Wuhan Doctor Speaks Out Against Authorities," *Guardian*, March 11, 2020, https://www.theguardian.com/world/2020/mar/11/coronavirus-wuhan -doctor-ai-fen-speaks-out-against-authorities.

2. Ellen G. White, "Our Words," *Advent Review and Sabbath Herald*, February 16, 1897, 92 [1].

3. This section is partially based on Gerald A. Klingbeil, "In the Wilderness: The Epidemic," *Adventist Review*, March 21, 2013, 26–28, https://www.adventistreview.org/2013-1508-26.

4. R. Dennis Cole, *Numbers*, New American Commentary, vol. 3B (Nashville, TN: B & H Pub., 2000), 179.

5. Roy B. Zuck, "A Theology of Proverbs," in *Learning From the Sages: Selected Studies on the Book of Proverbs*, ed. Roy B. Zuck (Grand Rapids, MI: Baker Books, 1995), 99.

6. See Bruce K. Waltke, *The Book of Proverbs: Chapters 1-15*, New International Commentary on the Old Testament (Grand Rapids, MI: Eerdmans, 2004), 536, 537.

Three

The Root of Restlessness

The sinking of the "unsinkable" RMS *Titanic* on her maiden voyage in 1912, due to a collision with an iceberg, caused the loss of about fifteen hundred lives. Based on the testimony of witnesses, the sea was unusually calm that night, making it more difficult to recognize the breaking of water at the base of an iceberg.[1] Since about 90 percent of an iceberg is invisible below the surface of the water,[2] the naval officers on the bridge of the *Titanic* were not able to recognize the dangerous iceberg fast enough and reduce their speed and course, ultimately leading to the catastrophic sinking.

We get it when we hear the idiomatic expression "the tip of the iceberg." It tells us that there is a visible hint of a problem, pointing to a much larger underlying issue.

Restlessness often functions as "the tip of the iceberg" in our lives, but we may not always recognize the underlying problem causing this restlessness. We mostly see what is apparent. When we look more carefully, we may see slightly beyond the apparent. Perfect vision, however, is twenty-twenty vision, with no blind spots or cataracts. Gaining this vision in our spiritual lives requires outside help.

Issue—getting to the root of rebellion

The fourth-century church father Augustine of Hippo is recorded as saying, "It was pride that changed angels into devils; it is humility that makes men as angels."[3] The Bible tells us that ambition and pride were the underlying motives leading to Lucifer's fall. We learn this from Isaiah's oracle depicting the fall of the king of Babylon (Isaiah 14). The highly evocative language of the passage suggests that Isaiah's prophetic vision went beyond historical events to metaphysical realities, pointing back to the fall of a created celestial being that coveted God's authority and wanted to be like God:[4]

"I will ascend into heaven,
I will exalt my throne above the stars of God;
I will also sit on the mount of the congregation
On the farthest sides of the north;
I will ascend above the heights of the clouds,
I will be like the Most High" (Isaiah 14:13, 14, NKJV).

Pride and self-exaltation caused Lucifer, the son of the morning, to rebel against his Creator. He wanted to be as great, or greater, than the One who can create worlds and galaxies by a simple word.

Pride lies right at the heart of the great controversy. "Pride in his own glory nourished the desire for supremacy," writes Ellen White. "The high honors conferred upon Lucifer were not appreciated as the gift of God and called forth no gratitude to the Creator. He gloried in his brightness and exaltation, and aspired to be equal with God."[5]

It was pride and ambition that prompted Lucifer to complain of the government of God, and to seek the overthrow of the order which had been established in heaven. Since his fall it has been his object to infuse the same spirit of envy and discontent, the same ambition for position and honor, into the minds of men. . . .

Do not the same evils still exist that lay at the foundation of

Korah's ruin? Pride and ambition are widespread; and when these are cherished, they open the door to envy, and a striving for supremacy; the soul is alienated from God, and unconsciously drawn into the ranks of Satan.[6]

Pride and selfishness lie right at the root of restlessness and ambition. We can see them when we look carefully into a mirror. Once we have recognized them, we may be tempted to self-medicate by trying to be "good," making every effort to give God a hand when it comes to our salvation. In fact, that is another form of pride, for we can always point to our good efforts, even though we may not make the grade. But this approach entices us to treat symptoms instead of root causes. Ultimately, we do not know who we really are and the real condition of our hearts.

Worldview—so who am I really?

Throughout history, we have wrestled with the question of who we really are. Deep down in our hearts, are we really good, or are we really bad? Are we wicked from the moment we are born, or do we come into the world as a clean slate and our experiences and choices in life make us good or bad? The phrase "nature versus nurture" summarizes these two extremes well. Some schools of thought have taught that we are naturally wicked from the moment of conception, while more modern philosophies have taught that with innocence comes goodness and that we are really all good at heart. Other philosophical positions have tried to avoid the question altogether and argue that good and bad are just social constructs. The Holocaust and the many horrendous genocides of the twentieth century, however, have made it difficult to explain away the presence of evil.

The Bible answers the question of who we are in a different way. We were created in the image of God (see Genesis 1:26, 27). Creation, including our first parents, was "very good" (verse 31). Yet after Adam and Eve chose to disobey, sin penetrated our DNA, and together with our eye color, we inherited the virus of sin. Without a cure, we were doomed. Sin, openly or quietly, goes about destroying the image of God in us until nothing good remains. The effects of the sin virus are much more evident in some than in others by the way that they behave, but in reality, all of us are sinners (Romans 3:9–20).

When we understand this, we realize that we do not have to keep looking within ourselves to find out who we are. What we need to know is who God is. Although we recognize that we are born with sin's virus, we can also know that Jesus paid for the cure and that He sees potential in us that we cannot even begin to understand. Only when we know and internalize this truth will our restlessness cease.

Digging deep—we all sit in the same boat
In Luke 18:9–14, Jesus tells a simple story about two men—a Pharisee and a tax collector—who go to the temple to pray. It is a story about self-discovery or, at the very least, self-evaluation. Both men tell God about who they think they are. The Pharisee and the tax collector pray short prayers, and then Jesus makes a value judgment call, pronouncing the tax collector justified!

How does this short story make us feel? Do we identify with the Pharisee or the tax collector? Most of us would hate to be labeled a Pharisee.

Being a Pharisee has become idiomatic for being a hypocrite. Jesus had little good to say about them. "Woe to you, teachers of the law and Pharisees, you hypocrites! You are like whitewashed tombs, which look beautiful on the outside but on the inside are full of the bones of the dead and everything unclean" (Matthew 23:27). That is just one accusation among many in that chapter. They were also the ones who systematically set out to kill the Son of God. No one wants to be a Pharisee.

So do we identify with the tax collector? Are we cheats? Have we turned traitor to our own people? Do people spit when they see us coming? Would we consider ourselves in the same moral league as prostitutes, murderers, drug dealers, or child abusers? Don't we wish that

The Root of Restlessness

Jesus had a third group in this parable that we could feel more comfortable with? Let us have a closer look at the prayers of the two men.

The Pharisee begins his prayer as every good prayer should begin—with praise. But this is praise with a twist. Instead of praising God for being God, he says, "God, I thank you that I am not like other people—robbers, evildoers, adulterers—or even like this tax collector" (Luke 18:11). Maybe he just cannot think of any bad things that he has done lately. He grew up in the church and never did drugs, went clubbing, or suffered serious hangovers.

Generally, looking to others to find out who we are or what lurks beneath the surface is risky as we can always find someone who is worse than we are. In this comparison, we will always look better by default.

The Pharisee thanks God that he is a pretty good man and then goes on to recite the evidence for this goodness. He fasts not just once a week, which would be impressive, but twice. Then he mentions his tithe paying, which, based on other statements of Jesus (e.g., Matthew 23:23), was quite a feat as it involved much more than simply giving 10 percent of his profits. He paid attention to the details and even took the trouble to tithe all the herbs used in his house!

Yet, in Jesus' evaluation, it is not good enough!

The tax collector, in contrast, has a lot less to say. He is, after all, a tax collector, and everyone, including the tax collector himself, knows what that means. He knows that he is the lowest of the low. He knows that he has nothing to be proud of. He has no list of good things done to offset the bad things. He does not have to look to others. He knows who he is. And yet he also seems to have some idea of who God is. Even though he knows who he is, he still ventures into the temple, and although he stands right at the back with a bowed head, he is ready to brave the looks and comments of all the better people in the temple because he really seems to think that God will hear him. His prayer is simple and to the point. Beating his chest as a sign of repentance, he cries, "God, have mercy on me, a sinner" (Luke 18:13).

In this parable, Jesus did not seem to think there could be a third category. Through the Pharisee and the tax collector, He tells us that in God's eyes, the world is not really divided into good and bad. Rather, the dividing line separates those who know that they need God's help and those who refuse to acknowledge that they need His salvation and restlessly strive to make it on their own.

Implications—we are divided
Fifty governments attended the United Nations Conference on International Organization in San Francisco, California, starting on April 25, 1945, several weeks before World War II ended in Europe with the unconditional surrender of Germany on May 8.[7] The delegates had high hopes of establishing an international entity and framework that would forever eliminate the danger of another world war. Sadly, these high hopes have not become a reality. Few days, if any, have gone by since 1946 when there was not at least one active war (including civil wars and regional wars).[8] The fact is, fallen human nature divides humanity. Selfishness, ambition, and pride lead to conflict and division. We are divided by gender, race, economic status, and education. These divisions not only affect the relationships between nations and tribes but also influence couples and families. While we seek to cross divides and mend the pain of separation, we realize that this requires an effort that goes beyond human capabilities. Like the postexilic community living in Jerusalem, facing conflict and antagonism all around them (Ezra 4), we would do well to remember God's special message to Zerubbabel, the governor who had led the first group of returnees home from Babylon: "This is the word of the LORD to Zerubbabel: 'Not by might nor by power, but by my Spirit,' says the LORD Almighty" (Zechariah 4:6). This Spirit-driven transformation offers a good starting point.

Take a breather—time for some healthy self-discovery
Teenagers are not the only ones who struggle to know who they really are. Most of us wonder about this at different moments in our lives.

God's Word offers some encouraging insights, and we would do well to remember these affirmations—even when we try to make sense of the world and our place in it.

> *For you created my inmost being;*
> *you knit me together in my mother's womb.*
> *I praise you because I am fearfully and wonderfully made;*
> *your works are wonderful,*
> *I know that full well (Psalm 139:13, 14).*

We are wanted and we are created—that is the starting point of our journey with God. We are not accidents or mishaps. God made us, and He made us wonderfully. In spite of our rebellious DNA, He is still invested heavily in us. He knows us and loves us in spite of what we have done.

"But you are a chosen people, a royal priesthood, a holy nation, God's special possession, that you may declare the praises of him who called you out of darkness into his wonderful light" (1 Peter 2:9). This sounds like a big statement. Peter reminds his readers that they are not alone. While we often define ourselves as individuals, we are really part of God's bigger master plan. He has chosen us. We are to extend His blessings to others (as the Old Testament priests did). We may share in His holiness, which is the opposite of our selfishness. We are His possessions by creation and salvation. All of these facts are meant to make us praise Him who transformed our darkness into a bright and shiny light.

"I no longer call you servants, because a servant does not know his master's business. Instead, I have called you friends, for everything that I learned from my Father I have made known to you" (John 15:15). Most of us do not get the radical nature of this statement that Jesus made to His disciples just prior to His betrayal. The original Greek text uses the noun *doulos*, which means literally "slave." This was not a reference to an employee or a business partner. In Jesus, God moved us from

servanthood and slavery to friendship. While there are references to God's friendship in the Old Testament (e.g., Abraham is called "the friend of God" in James 2:23, NKJV), Jesus offers us a new relationship with Himself. We tell our children to choose their friends wisely. Jesus chose us as friends, knowing full well who we really are.

" 'For I know the plans I have for you,' declares the LORD, 'plans to prosper you and not to harm you, plans to give you hope and a future' " (Jeremiah 29:11). God's plans (or "thoughts" as in the NKJV) for His people in Jeremiah's time were well designed. While exile was horrible, it was limited to a relatively short period. God's thoughts saw beyond the current reality and anticipated many new beginnings, ultimately leading to the coming of the Messiah. What would happen if we could be convinced that God's plans for us are truly good?

---

1. *Encyclopaedia Britannica Online*, s.v. "Titanic," by Amy Tikkanen, last updated October 15, 2020, https://www.britannica.com/topic/Titanic.

2. Wikipedia, s.v. "iceberg," last modified October 25, 2020, https://en.wikipedia.org /wiki/Iceberg.

3. The statement is attributed to Augustine of Hippo in *Manipulus florum*, comp. Thomas Hibernicus. The statement in Latin is "Humilitas homines sanctis angelis similes facit, et superbia ex angelis demones facit." "Superbia i," Electronic *Manipulus florum* Project, Wilfrid Laurier University, accessed November 10, 2020, http://web.wlu.ca/history/cnighman /MFfontes/SuperbiaI.pdf.

4. José Maria Bertoluci's doctoral dissertation offers strong evidence that the language used in Isaiah 14 and Ezekiel 28 transcends the earthly realm and points to a much larger context— that is, the beginning of the cosmic conflict. José Maria Bertoluci, "The Son of the Morning and the Guardian Cherub in the Context of the Controversy Between Good and Evil" (ThD diss., Andrews University, 1985).

5. Ellen G. White, *The Great Controversy* (Mountain View, CA: Pacific Press®, 1950), 495.

6. Ellen G. White, *Patriarchs and Prophets* (Mountain View, CA: Pacific Press®, 1958), 403, 404.

7. Wikipedia, s.v. "United Nations," last modified October 27, 2020, https://en.wikipedia .org/wiki/United_Nations; Wikipedia, s.v. "World War II," last modified October 29, 2020, https://en.wikipedia.org/wiki/World_War_II.

8. A helpful resource with relevant data can be found in the infographics by Max Roser, "War and Peace," Our World in Data, accessed November 10, 2020, https://ourworldindata .org/war-and-peace.

Four

The Cost of Rest

In the 1980s, a woman bought a ring for £10 (US$12.30) at a boot sale (similar to a flea market in America). The ring had a stone about the size of a peppermint, and because of the price, the lady assumed that it was made of glass. Thinking that the ring was a costume piece, she wore it a couple of times but kept it mostly in a drawer. Curious about its history and value, she took it to Sotheby's auction house in London in 2017. It turns out that when the ring was evaluated by experts, it was found to have a 26.29-carat diamond. The ring sold for £656,750 (US$810,055).

How is it possible to mistake an enormous diamond for a piece of glass for more than thirty years? we wonder. According to experts, it is quite easy to overlook a genuine diamond because large diamonds are so rare.[1] It would be easy to assume that a stone was not very valuable and overlook its extreme strength and flashing beauty just because one doesn't expect it to be so costly. If all we expect to see is glass, we will not be open to seeing a diamond and its true value. We will need outside help to make us look at the diamond differently.

Issue—free but not cheap

We love a discount and enjoy paying less for more. This is probably most evident in the clothing industry. We often throw away good clothes because we decide that they are somehow out of fashion and then set off to find a bargain. Finding a clothing item at a fraction of the cost often brings a thrill, albeit a short-lived one. For the most part, we do not seem to appreciate these bargains. Few of us mend holes or try to get stains out.

Although clothing prices have come down in recent decades, becoming relatively cheap, someone always pays. Fast fashion requires short production cycles and spur-of-the-moment buying decisions by the consumer. It also means a constant onslaught of advertising, which seeks to convince us that fashion has moved on and that we are unfashionable. Ultimately, it is a model that is completely unsustainable, encouraging overconsumption and generating excessive waste.[2] Beyond the wasted resources, it also affects lives directly. Factory workers (mostly women) in developing countries put in long hours, often in unsafe work environments, for very little pay.

Because salvation is free, we often treat it like fast fashion. We do not seem to realize that this wonderful gift is not cheap, even though it is free. It comes with a most expensive price tag.

There is a cost to everything we do and want. True rest also has a cost. While the spin doctors of self-help media want us to believe that we can determine our own destinies and that rest is just a matter of choice and planning, we realize, at least when we consider this honestly, our inability to bring true rest to our hearts, for true rest is entwined in salvation. The fourth-century church father Augustine put it succinctly in his famous *Confessions* as he considered God's grace: "You have made us for yourself, and our hearts are restless until they can find peace [rest] in you."[3] It is only in appreciation of the gift of salvation that we can find rest.

Worldview—more than head knowledge

There are so many things we can know on an intellectual level, but this knowledge may mean little to us. Knowing that our parents love us is important, but sometimes, especially as teenagers, we may have found it hard to understand this love. We may have had little understanding of the financial sacrifices our parents made for us. We may have regarded their rules as restrictive and could not understand why they struggled to sleep and worried when we were out late at night. We have no way of properly valuing this extremely expensive love (*physically*, just think of childbirth; *mentally*, trying to understand and anticipate what your child needs; *emotionally*, being quite prepared to die for your child). While a deeper appreciation of our parents' love normally comes with maturity, many of us only begin to understand and appreciate our parents' love when we ourselves become parents.

Understanding salvation can be equally daunting. We have nothing with which to compare this expensive gift and may have difficulty understanding and internalizing it. This is why God invites us to experience, on a much smaller level, what He has done for us through our relationships with others. Jesus taught us to pray, "Forgive us our debts, as we forgive our debtors" (Matthew 6:12, NKJV). He also said, "Love your enemies, bless those who curse you, do good to those who hate you, and pray for those who spitefully use you and persecute you, that you may be sons of your Father in heaven" (Matthew 5:44, 45, NKJV). As we forgive others, we begin to realize that we are forgiven. As we try to be a blessing to those who do not appreciate us, we begin to understand how God has loved us in spite of our behavior toward Him.

These hands-on experiences help us begin to understand the depth of salvation and some of its immense cost. And then something breaks in us, and we change. We become God's loudspeakers. We do not attempt to self-repair (whatever that means) or autoimprove (even incrementally). Our broken spirits—our contrite hearts—are enough praise for God, and they are beams of light that can be seen by the world surrounding us. Our experience of being forgiven attracts those searching for forgiveness (1 John 1:9).

Digging deep—our tutor

Sin is costly and causes disruption. It also generates restlessness deep down in our hearts. We intuitively know that we need something more. The biblical narrative connecting Eden to the new earth is full of stories that illustrate the destructive force of sin while, at the same time, highlighting God's abundant grace and His commitment to save His fallen creation. Right in the middle of all this, we find the law. The law is not something disconnected from God. The formal giving of the law on Mount Sinai was closely associated with God's self-revelation. God's law is intimately connected to His character, for it makes explicit the values and principles of the Lawgiver that have existed from eternity.

The question of the law became a focal point within Judaism, especially following the exile in Babylon. Israel's prophets had often pointed to the people's transgressions of God's law: their idolatry (Isaiah 44:9–20; Psalm 135:15–18), reliance on political powers other than the Lord (Isaiah 30:1–5; Jeremiah 2:18, 36), Sabbath keeping (Jeremiah 17:21–25; Ezekiel 20:11–16), and many more. But they had spoken most urgently against the abuse of the powerless, the disregard of justice, and the ill-treatment of orphans and widows that were under His specific care (Jeremiah 22:3; Zechariah 7:10; Amos 2:6–8; Micah 6:11, 12; 7:2–6).

At the time of Jesus, rabbis, legal scholars, and others had created a legal superstructure that had little in common with the simplicity and depth of the expression of God's character as found in the Ten Commandments. The question of the role of the law in religious life was debated heatedly in first-century Judaism.

Jesus stepped right into this debate when He offered an alternative view of the law that was intended to lead His audience back to the original. In His sermon on the mount, He repeatedly engages with the Old Testament revelation of the law: "You have heard that it was said to those of old, 'You shall not murder, and whoever murders will be in danger of the judgment.' But I say to you that whoever is angry with his brother without a cause shall be in danger of the judgment. And whoever says to his brother, 'Raca!' [meaning "empty head" in Aramaic] shall be in danger of the council. But whoever says, 'You fool!' shall be in danger of hell fire" (Matthew 5:21, 22, NKJV).

While most of His audience focused on the externals of a given law, Jesus pointed to the bigger principle and motivation of the law. How many times have we become guilty of "murdering" our neighbors when we considered them idiotic, stupid, or silly? We shudder as we do the mental math, and that's when Jesus tells us, "Do not think that I came to destroy the Law or the Prophets. I did not come to destroy but to fulfill" (verse 17, NKJV). Jesus gives us a quick glimpse of the fuller meaning of God's law; the Lawgiver offers a small window into the heart of God—His character.

Paul's letter to the Galatians tackles some of these issues. Galatians also has a long trajectory in Adventist discourse, especially in the discussion about the significance—both historically and theologically—of the 1888 General Conference Session in Minneapolis.[4] While this is not the place to offer an in-depth discussion of the issues that caused many of the delegates of the 1888 General Conference Session sleepless nights, we should pay attention to Paul's argument. In Galatians 2:21, Paul states, "I do not set aside the grace of God, for if righteousness could be gained through the law, Christ died for nothing!" For Paul, the Cross and the law are inseparably connected. He continues his argument in the following verses: "You foolish Galatians! Who has bewitched you? Before your very eyes Jesus Christ was clearly portrayed as crucified. I would like to learn just one thing from you: Did you receive the Spirit by the works of the law, or by believing what you heard? Are you so foolish? After beginning by means of the Spirit, are you now trying to finish by means of the flesh?" (Galatians 3:1–3).

The church members living in the province of Galatia had started their faith journey with a solid focus on the Cross and salvation by faith in Jesus. Paul admonishes them not to follow a "different gospel" (Galatians 1:6) now, promoted by those who want to "pervert the gospel of Christ" (verse 7).

While the law clearly unmasks the fallen human condition, it is not through keeping the law that we are saved. It is the cross and the righteousness of Christ that is given in exchange for our sins and guilt. The law is God's way of making our need evident and thus leading us to look at the cross and our Savior for the gift of salvation. In Galatians 3:24, Paul describes this role of the law by the Greek noun *paidagogos*, meaning "tutor" or "guardian." Well-to-do citizens living in the first century AD had slaves who looked after their children and helped with their education. Some of these slaves may have been known for their kindness, but the predominant sense of the term is that they disciplined and protected the child.[5] The English term *pedagogy* is connected to this term. This tutor (i.e., the law) leads us to Christ, for the law documents our sinfulness. It cannot change our situation, for we need a Savior—not a tutor or guardian. The root of our restlessness is pride and rebellion. The law illustrates the immense cost associated with our sin and our inability to contribute anything to pay the cost. The Cross eliminates any doubt in the entire universe about God's character and love. It offers us the only way to truly find rest.

Implications—no cheap grace
Some of us, at times, struggle with the concept of salvation. We recognize that the price of forgiveness was costly and exorbitant. We know the terrible suffering that Jesus experienced to stand in our stead. We appreciate grace, and we even tell those around us about this marvelous grace that saves us. But when it is our turn to receive grace and forgiveness, we begin to wonder about our role in this process. We camouflage this unease by serious theological discussions about justification and sanctification. Could it be that I just have to ask for

forgiveness and then trust in His grace? Isn't this cheap grace, peddled by so many who seem to buy into the "once saved, always saved" idea in which grace just seems to give us license to keep on sinning? Or is salvation a way to avoid the consequences of our actions while continuing to "enjoy" the sins themselves?

One of the best examples of salvation and the expense of the gift can be found in the life of David. David repented of his sins of adultery and murder when confronted by the prophet Nathan, but his repentance did not mean that all the consequences of his sins magically disappeared. David could not repair the tremendous damage that had been done through his acts or his example to his family. Uriah the Hittite had been killed, and David's newborn child died as a result. David suffered the consequences of his decisions and actions, and his moral standing before his people and his children weakened tremendously. The last part of his reign included many setbacks and rebellions.

Yet David knew that he had been forgiven. He knew that he needed to trust by faith that one day the true Lamb of God would come and stand in his place. This was no cheap grace. He had seen firsthand what damage his sins had done, and he could never consider God's grace cheap. This understanding of God's grace transformed him. He understood that without a daily close connection with God, given an opportunity, he was literally capable of anything—including murder. He understood as never before that his only hope was to cling to God. A true understanding of the immense cost of salvation and a complete surrender to grace are the best ways of guarding against "cheap grace."

Take a breather—trust Him completely

There are many entry points for doubt to enter our minds. We may doubt our worthiness, we may doubt God's power, we may even doubt His presence, but we should never doubt His grace, for the Cross continues to speak loudly across millennia. The God who is willing to hang on a cross and die, bearing the sins and guilt of His rebellious creation, is more than willing and capable of renewing our hearts. Here are three Bible references that need to be on our minds during dark times.

"For by grace you have been saved through faith, and this is not your own doing; it is the gift of God—not the result of works, so that no one may boast. For we are what he has made us, created in Christ Jesus for good works, which God prepared beforehand to be our way of life" (Ephesians 2:8–10, NRSV). Costly grace stands at the beginning; divine grace brings up the rear; and in between, there is God's handiwork made visible in our lives.

"The LORD bless you
   and keep you;
the LORD make his face shine on you
   and be gracious to you;
the LORD turn his face toward you
   and give you peace" (Numbers 6:24–26).

This timeless blessing reminds us that our peace and well-being are a result of God's blessings. His face is squarely set toward us.

"For the grace of God has appeared that offers salvation to all people. It teaches us to say 'No' to ungodliness and worldly passions, and to live self-controlled, upright and godly lives in this present age" (Titus 2:11, 12). God's grace did not just appear out of nowhere. His timing was perfect, and His offering is available to all people. Once we understand this, we commit to living God-centered lives that will point back to the Giver of all good gifts.

---

1. Levi Higgs, "The Precious Jewels Hidden in Flea Markets and Garage Sales," *Daily Beast*, last updated February 11, 2018, https://www.thedailybeast.com/the-precious-jewels-hidden-in-flea-markets-and-garage-sales.

2. A brief introduction to fast fashion can be found in Alex Crumbie, "What Is Fast Fashion and Why Is It a Problem?" *Ethical Consumer*, September 5, 2019, https://www.ethicalconsumer

.org/fashion-clothing/what-fast-fashion-why-it-problem.

3. Rex Warner, trans., *The Confessions of Saint Augustine* (New York: Signet Classic, 2001), 1.

4. For a brief, albeit helpful, introduction to the topic, we recommend George R. Knight, "What Happened in 1888? A Historical Account of a Very Historic Event," *Adventist Review*, October 10, 2013, https://www.adventistreview.org/2013-1528-p16. Cf., also in the same issue, Merlin Burt, "The Faith of Jesus: The Doctrinal Legacy of 1888," *Adventist Review*, October 10, 2013, https://www.adventistreview.org/2013-1528-p24.

5. Timothy George, *Galatians*, New American Commentary, vol. 30 (Nashville, TN: B & H Pub., 1994), 265.

Five

Come Unto Me

For some, surrender is not easy. Shoichi Yokoi was this type of person. While others graduated from college, helped to rebuild their country, married, and had children, he remained at war, completely unaware that World War II had ended. Yokoi had been part of the Japanese forces that captured the island of Guam in 1941. After three years of Japanese occupation, the United States retook the island. Yokoi was left behind by the retreating Japanese army and went into hiding rather than surrender to the Allies. For the next twenty-eight years, he hid in the jungle, scavenging food and just trying to survive undetected. Finally, in 1972, he was discovered by local hunters. When he was found, he was terrified and tried to fight the hunters off, still thinking that his life was in danger. They managed to subdue him and take him back to civilization, where he was subsequently discharged and sent home to Japan. For Yokoi, the war had finally ended.[1]

Issue—surrender to win

"Surrender to win," James Butler was told at Narcotics Anonymous. For Butler, surrender was hard. As an addict, he knew that alcohol and cocaine were draining the life out of him. He knew that either substance could kill him soon, yet he struggled to surrender. When he finally did, he recalls, "Paradoxically, all that I lost in surrender was my own helplessness. In its place, I gained freedom to act out of my true self-interest, even if it was only a day or a minute at a time." He also states, "Day by day I was throwing up the white flag of surrender—not to my craving but to a program of recovery. I was learning that I couldn't save myself, and that I needed support from a community and my Higher Power to stay sober."[2]

Surrendering is one of the hardest things human beings do. We desperately hang on to control of our lives, even in the face of clear evidence that we are messing up beyond repair. Sometimes events in our lives push us past our limits, and we struggle desperately with the realization that we cannot control the outcome. We feel that surrender is somehow connected with defeat and weakness, yet it is only in surrender that we can find rest. We have to take Jesus up on His invitation (Matthew 11:28) and set ourselves adrift in the promise of His love and power, surrendering the fight and entering His rest.

Worldview—the path to salvation
The idea of a Savior is foreign to many of the world's major religions.

Islam does not propagate the need for a Savior; believers can avoid hell by following the guidance of Allah in doing good and avoiding evil.[3]

In Hinduism, salvation is not found in deliverance from particular sins or a sinful state but rather is equivalent to reaching a state of enlightenment and ultimate freedom from the cycle of death and reincarnation by becoming complete. There are many ways to reach this freedom. One can do good deeds, perform religious ceremonies, meditate, use yoga, and employ the mind to understand the universe. Each of these ways requires a person to do certain things.[4]

In Buddhism, too, the focus is on breaking away from the cycle of birth and death by gaining enlightenment. Finding this requires effort and concentrated willpower over many lifetimes.[5]

In contrast, Jesus simply calls us to come. We do not have to wait until we meet a certain standard to come. We do not have to be good to qualify. We come as we are—even though Jesus never leaves us as we were. Through His Spirit, Jesus offers us a lifetime process of transformation to re-create in us the person He originally meant us to be.

Digging deep—*come* can mean many things

The imperative *come* can have many meanings. It can refer to a friendly invitation to move from point A to point B. When we receive a message from a good friend asking us to "come" to her birthday party, we immediately understand that she wants us to be present physically, which requires movement. We need to leave our home, get into our car, take a bus, catch a plane, or just walk for fifteen minutes to physically reach our friend's place. A simple "come" moves us to action.

At the same time, our friend's "come" is not simply an invitation to relocate physically. It is also an expression of friendship, trust, and affection. It tells us that we are wanted and appreciated. Our presence will make the event a success. Friendship is expressed by a gentle and friendly "come."

Now imagine a different type of *come*. A dog gets off his leash and is racing toward a busy road; his eyes are on a rabbit desperately trying to get away. The frantic and upset owner gives chase and keeps shouting, "Come—right now!" We do not need to watch a video to imagine the soundtrack. The angry owner's "come" sounds very different from the "come" in the invitation to our friend's birthday. Tone, facial expression, volume, and the larger context can make a significant difference.

God's "come" in Scripture is similarly multifaceted. He says "come" to individuals and groups. "Come" presupposes a prior relationship. We need to know the One who invites us to come. God calls Moses, "Come now, therefore, and I will send you to Pharaoh that you may bring My people, the children of Israel, out of Egypt" (Exodus 3:10,

NKJV). This "come" appears in the context of God's coming down (verse 8) to deliver His people suffering in slavery after Israel's cries came before God (verse 9). Moses initially does not want to "come" and go to Pharaoh as Israel's leader and God's representative. Ultimately, however, he responds to God's invitation and is willing to go. We go after we have come to Jesus.

God often said "come" to His people in Old Testament times. Often this meant a conscious decision to return to God and His worship instead of following other gods. Isaiah 1:18 offers an intriguing window into God's engagement with His people:

> "Come now, and let us reason together,"
> Says the LORD,
> "Though your sins are like scarlet,
> They shall be as white as snow;
> Though they are red like crimson,
> They shall be as wool" (NKJV).

Scholars have recognized the legal overtones of the language used in this verse.[6] The Hebrew word *yakakh*, which is translated as "and let us reason" here, is often used in the context of judgment (e.g., Genesis 31:37; Job 23:7; Isaiah 11:4). God lays out Israel's actions that have voided their covenant with Him, including Israel's perverted worship and adherence to empty forms that do not entail a heart change (Isaiah 1:10–15). Then He suggests to them, beginning in verses 16 and 17, a number of imperatives for a radical change of heart: washing, putting away evil doings, ceasing to do evil, and then, learning to do good, seeking justice, rebuking the oppressor, defending the fatherless, and pleading for the widow. The invitation to come and enter into a legal conversation comes right at the end of God's passionate plea.

God's "come" often requires courage and trust. We need to step out of our comfort zones and surrender completely to Him instead of trusting in our own abilities. When Peter steps out of the relative safety of a boat in the midst of a terrifying storm after Jesus tells him, "Come" (Matthew 14:29), and walks upon the water toward the Master, he must feel elation and excitement for a few moments. Yes, his faith wavers when he triumphantly looks back at his companions in the boat, for Peter loses sight of Jesus.[7] His cry for help when he begins to sink is heard by Jesus. Matthew records that "immediately Jesus stretched out His hand and caught him" (verse 31, NKJV). When we respond to God's "come," we are often faced with critical decisions that require us to focus on first things first. We need to surrender.

Among the hundreds of references to God's "come," we should remember the last one, which is mentioned in Revelation 22. Those yearning for a new earth and a new heaven offer this Spirit-guided cry: "And the Spirit and the bride say, 'Come!' And let him who hears say, 'Come!' And let him who thirsts come. Whoever desires, let him take the water of life freely" (verse 17, NKJV). The cry of the bride, amplified by the Spirit, is "Come!" Those who have the ability to hear the Spirit's nudging cry, "Come!" Jesus, the Faithful Witness, responds in verse 20: "He who testifies to these things says, 'Surely I am coming quickly' " (NKJV).

New Testament scholar G. K. Beale offers these important insights: "Jesus' reaffirmation throughout the Apocalypse, 'Yes, I am coming quickly,' serves to confirm the validity of his testimony. That is, he assures the churches about the truth of the complete vision by guaranteeing that his final advent, which he promised at his first coming, will soon occur and thus bring to completion what he has revealed throughout the book."[8] This is the moment when our coming meets God's "come."

Implications—the ABCs of surrender
Don't procrastinate, come! We cannot afford to wait to see whether we can improve a bit before we surrender our lives to God. We must give up on the idea of self-improvement and come to Jesus as we are.

Although "the warfare against self is the greatest battle,"⁹ it is only by surrendering to God that we can find His offer of rest and renewal.

So on a practical level, what does surrender to God look like? Surrender is that moment when we realize that our strategies and coping mechanisms are futile and destructive. Surrender is the recognition that we are sick with the virus of sin. Surrender is the realization that more effort, thinking, and doing will not work. True surrender is the conscious decision to turn ourselves over to God.

Surrender does not mean that we vow to do better because we all know that we cannot control our thoughts or compulsions, tastes or deep yearnings. We can still surrender even if we know that we do not have strong willpower or we are struggling with some addiction or years of firmly established bad habits. Surrender is letting go of broken promises and hopeless attempts. *Surrender is the realization that we do not know how to.* Although we do not know how to change our hearts or break free from things that have a hold on us, we can choose to surrender. "You can give Him your will; He will then work in you to will and to do according to His good pleasure. Thus your whole nature will be brought under the control of the Spirit of Christ; your affections will be centered upon Him, your thoughts will be in harmony with Him."¹⁰

In surrendering ourselves to God, we will also have to take a hard look at everything that separates us from Him (Luke 13:3). Surrender is never a 50-percent or 75-percent deal. Surrender is not surrender unless it is 100 percent. We must abandon everything that is an idol in our lives. This can include relationships, objects, dreams, addictions, or pleasures that lure our hearts away from Jesus. They all need to be given to God. God really loves us, and our surrender, although a painful struggle with self, is not the drudgery that many of us fear. God does not want us to give up anything that will be for our eternal best interest, and He offers us lives that are so much better than any we could try to hang on to ourselves (John 10:10). The missionary Jim Elliot, who gave his life to reach the Huaorani people of Ecuador, understood surrender. In his journal, he penned the following: "He is no fool who gives what he cannot keep to gain that which he cannot lose."[11]

Take a breather—all to Jesus I surrender
Surrender begins with submission. We recognize our need and willingly hand over the keys to our hearts and wills. Consider these three biblical texts, among hundreds, that offer practical help as we struggle with the "how" of surrender.

"Therefore submit to God. Resist the devil and he will flee from you. Draw near to God and He will draw near to you" (James 4:7, 8, NKJV). Submitting to God begins the process of surrender. Interestingly, "the [Greek] word *hypotassō*, 'submit,' is the opposite of the word *antitassomai*, 'oppose,' in the previous verse." James calls us to "stop resisting God in anything" and any part of our lives.[12] The next step is active resistance of the devil. While we cannot overcome him on our own, when we resist *and* draw near to God, God will draw close— and Satan will be on the run. Surrender to God begins with submitting our will to our heavenly Father.

"My son, give me your heart and let your eyes delight in my ways" (Proverbs 23:26). When we realize that we are God's children and that our divine Parent means well, we can give Him our hearts. The second half of this poetic line is always surprising. When we do, we will find delight in His ways in our lives. We will stand with open mouths, watching Him transform us.

"Therefore, I urge you, brothers and sisters, in view of God's mercy, to offer your bodies as a living sacrifice, holy and pleasing to God—this is your true and proper worship" (Romans 12:1). Paul's invitation to the Romans uses the familiar imagery of an offering. Usually, sacrifices were killed to function as an offering. But this one is different. It involves a "living sacrifice"; it requires full surrender, resulting in true worship.

Judson Van DeVenter wrote his most famous hymn in 1896: "I

Surrender All." It turns out that these lines were autobiographical. He later wrote,

> The song was written while I was conducting a meeting at East Palestine, Ohio, and in the home of George Sebring. . . . For some time, I had struggled between developing my talents in the field of art and going into full-time evangelistic work. At last the pivotal hour of my life came, and I surrendered all. A new day was ushered into my life. I became an evangelist and discovered down deep in my soul a talent hitherto unknown to me. God had hidden a song in my heart, and touching a tender chord, he caused me to sing.[13]

I will ever love and trust Him,
In His presence daily live;
I surrender all, I surrender all;
All to Thee, my blessed Savior,
I surrender all.[14]

---

1. For more details on the story, see Mike Lanchin, "Shoichi Yokoi, the Japanese Soldier Who Held Out in Guam," BBC, January 24, 2012, https://www.bbc.com/news/magazine-16681636.

2. James B., quoted in Anderson Spickard Jr., "Surrender," *Craving Brain* (blog), *Psychology Today*, May 8, 2019, https://www.psychologytoday.com/us/blog/the-craving-brain/201905/surrender.

3. "What Is Salvation in Islam?" [Christian Reformed Church] Network, last updated March 1, 2018, https://network.crcna.org/ecumenical-interfaith/what-salvation-islam.

4. James Stuart, "Path to Salvation of Hindus," Classroom, September 29, 2017, https://classroom.synonym.com/path-to-salvation-of-hindus-12085220.html.

5. K. Sri Dhammananda Maha Thera, "What Buddhists Believe: How to Save Yourself," BuddhaSasana, accessed October 29, 2020, https://www.budsas.org/ebud/whatbudbeliev/191.htm.

6. See, e.g., J. Alec Motyer, *The Prophecy of Isaiah* (Leicester, UK: InterVarsity, 1993), 47, 48.

7. Ellen G. White, *The Desire of Ages* (Mountain View, CA: Pacific Press®, 1940), 381.

8. G. K. Beale, *The Book of Revelation: A Commentary on the Greek Text*, New International Greek Testament Commentary (Grand Rapids, MI: Eerdmans, 1999), 1155.

9. Ellen G. White, *Steps to Christ* (Washington, DC: Review and Herald®, 1908), 43.

10. White, 47.

11. Jim Elliot, quoted in Kevin Halloran, "Jim Elliot's Journal Entry With 'He Is No Fool. . .' Quote," *Anchored in Christ* (blog), October 28, 2013, https://www.kevinhalloran .net/jim-elliot-quote-he-is-no-fool/.

12. Kurt A. Richardson, *James*, New American Commentary, vol. 36 (Nashville, TN: B & H Pub., 1997), 183.

13. "History of Hymns: 'I Surrender All,' " Discipleship Ministries, July 1, 2012, https:// www.umcdiscipleship.org/resources/history-of-hymns-i-surrender-all.

14. 14. Judson W. Van De Venter, "I Surrender All" (1896).

Six

Finding Rest in Turbulent Family Ties

Scripture's faith heroes did not always have ideal relationships. Even our Adventist pioneers had their struggles. James and Ellen White's marriage and children were not perfect. Edson White, James and Ellen's second son, proved to be particularly difficult.[1] The young man married early and seemed to have a very spasmodic relationship with the fledgling Seventh-day Adventist Church, which his parents were instrumental in founding. One of his biggest problems was the way he spent money. He was careless and often in debt, resorting to quick ways of making money. He also had a public falling-out with the church over printing copyrights. His behavior caused his parents much embarrassment and strained his relationship with them, particularly with his father.

After James's death in 1881, Edson seemed to throw off any connections with the church and wrote to his mother that he had "no religious inclinations . . . in the least."[2] Heartbroken, Ellen often wrote to her son, pleading with him to give his life to God, seemingly with little success. Ellen White went on praying and writing him letters, never cutting off her love and tender concern for her prodigal son. Eventually, at the age of forty-four, Edson fully committed his life to

Jesus. He designed a steam paddleboat called the *Morning Star* and traveled up and down the Mississippi River to bring education and knowledge of Jesus to the impoverished former slaves of the South.

Issues—no one is an island
We get to choose some relationships in life, but many of those closest to us, such as our parents and siblings, we do not get to choose. While in some areas of the world there are multiple congregations to choose from, most places do not have that luxury, and we often have to live with some difficult people in our church family. Seeing that we serve a perfect God, we would all like to reflect this perfection in our families and church families, but the truth is that, in this sinful world, no one is perfect, and none of us have perfect families and perfect relationships. Some of us are blessed by parents, siblings, and other family members that reflect God's love, but many of us have to settle for less than the ideal. Family and church relationships are often complicated and painful. In the case of our church families, many of us solve this problem by simply not attending church anymore. But this is not a solution, and no one is an island—especially not spiritually. We need each other, as imperfect as we are, on our faith journey.

Although relationship problems can leave us restless, hurt, and carrying loads of emotional baggage, we want to find rest and avoid becoming conduits of pain and dysfunction for others. The good news is that even when others are trying to manipulate us or just see us as objects, we can refuse to treat them in kind because we realize that God knows us, that we are loved, and that we have value.

God has high ideals for our relationships, and so should we, but we should not be unrealistic about them. We must accept and work with the real, not the ideal. We must be ready to lower the pretenses and façades that we protect ourselves with, especially in our church families, and make ourselves vulnerable and willing to ask for help.

It is also good to remember that our real problems are not with other people but with the one who stands behind all hurts and misunderstandings—the one who specializes in causing maximum pain. We must remember that our relationships are miniature models of the great controversy between God and Satan, which has been raging throughout the ages. Every relationship must have growth dynamics, and Satan consistently throws curveballs into our relationships. When we remember this, we will be better braced to lean on God and view our relationships as opportunities for growth. We will not be so quick to bail out when we realize that we do not reach the ideal.

Some of our relationship problems are rooted in our poor choices, while others are caused by circumstances beyond our control. As we read the Bible, it is comforting to note that God's faith champions often fall short of their own and God's expectations. The people listed in Hebrews 11's faith Hall of Fame are not there because of their messy family relationships but in spite of them. These people learned—often the hard way—about faith, love, and trust in God as they wrestled with their relationship issues.

Worldview—between the ideal and the real

Things were so easy in the beginning. Adam and Eve were to care for the earth and the garden they had been placed in. Since they had been created in God's image and likeness, they would reflect God's goodness, His holiness, and ultimately, His character to all the creation surrounding them.[3]

It never happened. Sin separated the human family from God. The Fall brought pain, death, abuse, jealousy, violence, hunger for power and dominion, and so many more evil attitudes to this world. The descendants of Adam and Eve became their own worst enemies.

God had a plan to return His lost children to the Garden. He called a people to be His and shine His light in a dark world (Isaiah 49:6). He gave them signs and illustrations of His plan of salvation (think, for example, of the Sabbath or the sanctuary). His laws reflected His character and illustrated His kingdom's values in practical ways: how children should relate to their parents and vice versa;

how fidelity results in happy marriages; how murder, stealing, gossip, and coveting are destructive to the social fabric of the community. God admonished them to care for widows, orphans, outsiders, and those who are powerless and to administer justice fairly. (Deuteronomy 10:12–22 offers a good summary of these principles of God's law [cf. Exodus 22:16–31].)

Reality, however, looked different in biblical Israel. For hundreds of years, Israel's prophets spoke out against abuse and unethical behavior. The relationship between God and Israel was often dysfunctional.

> Her [Judah's] heads judge for a bribe,
> Her priests teach for pay,
> And her prophets divine for money.
> Yet they lean on the LORD, and say,
> "Is not the LORD among us?
> No harm can come upon us" (Micah 3:11, NKJV).

God repeatedly spoke through His prophets against the attitudes and actions of His people. "For if you [Judah] thoroughly amend your ways and your doings, if you thoroughly execute judgment between a man and his neighbor, if you do not oppress the stranger, the fatherless, and the widow, and do not shed innocent blood in this place, or walk after other gods to your hurt, then I will cause you to dwell in this place, in the land that I gave to your fathers forever and ever" (Jeremiah 7:5–7, NKJV).

The Israelites clearly struggled with idolatry (1 Kings 12:25–33; 16:29–33; etc.), but God's most recurring accusations involved their ethical lapses and their belief that unethical behavior could be balanced out by abundant sacrifices (Hosea 6:4–6; Micah 6:6–8). The God of Scripture cannot be manipulated by pious displays of religious action or lavish giving. Listen to the rush of His voice ringing right into the twenty-first century:

"I hate, I despise your feast days,
And I do not savor your sacred assemblies.
Though you offer Me burnt offerings and your grain offerings,
I will not accept them,
Nor will I regard your fattened peace offerings.
Take away from Me the noise of your songs,
For I will not hear the melody of your stringed instruments.
But let justice run down like water,
And righteousness like a mighty stream" (Amos 5:21–24, NKJV).

Digging deep—the power of covenant

Today, when two large companies want to merge, they need armies of lawyers who spend months drafting legal documents ranging from the letter of intent to the final acquisition agreement. They must take care of government regulations affecting the merger, work with unions on employment issues, consider the funding for retirement obligations, and much more.

In biblical times, two parties entered into a covenant by enacting a ritual involving a sacrificial animal that was cut into two halves. We find a good example of such a ritual in Genesis 15, accompanying the covenant between the Lord and Abraham. The elements of biblical covenant rituals included an introduction to both parties, a review of past interactions, the conditions of the covenant, and the consequences (blessings and curses) that would befall the party breaking the covenant.

Intriguingly, biblical covenants are always based on God's initiative. He initiates any covenant, He offers the assurance of the covenant, and He also highlights the future consequences of the covenant. In the case of Genesis 15, God initiates the conversation with Abraham (he is still called Abram in that chapter) by reassuring this man who left Ur to live like a defenseless stranger in Canaan: "Do not be afraid, Abram. I am your shield, your exceedingly great reward" (verse 1, NKJV; cf. verse 7). We would do well to remember that God's covenant with Abraham and his descendants is not based on Abraham's faith response (even though faith is required) but that it always begins with God's promise. In Abraham's case, this promise included offspring and land (verses 4, 5, 18–21). Other important covenants included God's covenant with Noah (Genesis 8:20–9:17), God's covenant with Israel at Mount Sinai (Exodus 19:5, 6; 20–23), and God's covenant with David (2 Samuel 7:1–17).

At the foundation of all of these expressions of God's desire to save humanity, however, lies His eternal covenant. The phrase "eternal [or everlasting] covenant" appears only once in the New Testament—in Hebrews 13:20. Adventist theologian Peter van Bemmelen notes, "It is evident, however, that the everlasting covenant that God established with Abraham and his seed, with the people of Israel, and with King David, finds its fulfillment in the person of Jesus of Nazareth."[4] This eternal covenant was founded on the agreement within the Trinity, laid before the foundation of the world, to save fallen humanity. This is also confirmed by Ellen White, who wrote in 1901: "The covenant of mercy was made before the foundation of the world. It has existed from all eternity, and is called the everlasting covenant. So surely as there never was a time when God was not, so surely there never was a moment when it was not the delight of the eternal mind to manifest His grace to humanity."[5]

Adventist systematic theologian Norman Gulley offers this helpful summary of biblical covenant theology:

It was God's intent that the covenants between Himself and humans reflect the reciprocal love within the inner-Trinitarian Being of God. On God's part, love for humans has never changed, but humans have for the most part failed to respond to this love. It is only within the context of God's everlasting love manifest in His everlasting covenant that we can best understand the old and the new covenants (or see the compatibility between the Sinai and new covenants). . . .

. . . On linguistic and theological grounds, subsequent covenants are a renewal of the original covenant of God with humans.
The new covenant is a renewal of the Sinai covenant, which is
itself a renewal of the covenant with Abraham, and all covenants
are a renewal of the original creation covenant.[6]

The reality of God's covenant people, as already noted above, was
far removed from God's ideal. Dysfunction reigned supreme, both in
God's Old Testament covenant people and in the early Christian
church (e.g., some of the narratives in Acts depict racial tensions
between Jewish Christians and Gentile Christians; the theological
conflicts, illustrated by Peter and Paul's clash in Antioch, as noted in
Galatians 2:11–21). In spite of these dysfunctions and challenges,
God's commitment to saving fallen humanity (including His people
and later His church) has been unwavering. God's love and grace lie
at the heart of His eternal, unchanging faithful covenant, offering us
a way home.

Implications—doing relationships God's way
How can we find rest when those closest to us seem set on making our
lives miserable? How can we survive dysfunctional families and a culture that emphasizes *I* and not *we*? We will have to learn to do something seemingly counterproductive: we must apply biblical principles
to all of our relationships, even when others are not fighting fair. And
although we can save ourselves from many painful detours by following biblical principles in our relationships, we may not always see the
results we want, even though this does not exempt us from behaving
and interacting as God would have us.

Practicing biblical principles in our relationships and accepting less
than ideal relationships does not mean that we can or should ever
accept any type of abuse, including sexual abuse or any emotional or
physical violence. Abuse is never to be part of any relationship
dynamic. It is not just a private matter to be resolved internally. It will

need outside help and intervention to break the cycle. Please get help!

Additionally, we cannot control the choices of others. We can, however, decide to live, love, and treat those around us in ways that will honor God.

Being a nominal Christian or a cultural Adventist will not help us to find rest in our relationships. To find rest, we each must make a personal decision to follow God. Even if our ancestors were spiritual giants—this is not transmitted genetically. Remember, God only has children—no grandchildren.

Take a breather—we can choose

There is no natural law suggesting that dysfunction automatically generates more dysfunction. We have choices, and God's Word invites us to make good choices.

"This day I call the heavens and the earth as witnesses against you that I have set before you life and death, blessings and curses. Now choose life, so that you and your children may live" (Deuteronomy 30:19). God did not create us as robots. We are able to choose between right and wrong. We have the power to choose life. In Moses' final words to his people, standing at the border to the Promised Land, he invites them to "choose life, so that you and your children may live" (verse 19). Our choices have long-lasting consequences.

"Now fear the LORD and serve him with all faithfulness. Throw away the gods your ancestors worshiped beyond the Euphrates River and in Egypt, and serve the LORD. But if serving the LORD seems undesirable to you, then choose for yourselves this day whom you will serve, whether the gods your ancestors served beyond the Euphrates, or the gods of the Amorites, in whose land you are living. But as for me and my household, we will serve the LORD" (Joshua 24:14, 15). At the end of a long military campaign, Joshua calls Israel's leaders to Shechem to renew the covenant with the Lord. He knows that when things go smoothly, we tend to go easy on our relationship with God. He first recalls the story of God's initial call to Abraham and his descendants and His liberation

of Israel from slavery in Egypt. He then puts before the people two choices: *you can serve the gods of our ancestors, or you can serve the Lord.* But that is not all. Joshua knows the power of example, and so he continues: "But as for me and my household, we will serve the Lord" (verse 15). When we choose God, we have already begun to break the bondage of dysfunction.

---

1. The following narrative is based on Paul B. Ricchiuti, *Four Boys in the White House: The Children of James and Ellen White* (Grantham, UK: Stanborough Press, 2008).

2. James Edson White to Ellen G. White, letter, May 18, 1893, 2, Ellen G. White Estate, http://ellenwhite.org/content/correspondence/white-je/002860pdf.

3. This section is based on Gerald A. Klingbeil, "Between the Ideal and the Real: We Often Struggle to Live God's Kingdom Values," *Adventist World*, March 2020, 11, https://www.adventistworld.org/between-the-ideal-and-the-real/.

4. Peter M. van Bemmelen, "The Everlasting Covenant," *Perspective Digest* 19, no. 4 (October 1, 2014), https://www.perspectivedigest.org/archive/19-4/the-everlasting-covenant.

5. Ellen G. White, "Spiritual Growth," *Signs of the Times*, June 12, 1901.

6. Norman R. Gulley, "The Two Covenants of Scripture Are Really One and the Same," *Perspective Digest* 19, no. 1 (January 1, 2014), https://www.perspectivedigest.org/archive/19-1/gods-everlasting-covenant.

Seven

Rest, Relationships, and Healing

It still is a chilling black-and-white image. The nine-year-old Vietnamese girl's mouth is wide open in a scream, her body a patchwork of burns, as she runs naked from a napalm-bomb attack. It has remained a powerful image since it made front-page news in 1972 during the Vietnam War and won Associated Press photographer Huynh Cong Ut a Pulitzer Prize.[1] The girl, Phan Thi Kim Phúc, was so badly burned that doctors thought she could not survive. Against the odds, she did survive and had to endure seventeen surgical procedures, including extensive skin grafts. Phan Thi Kim Phúc was in constant pain and remained angry at those who had dropped the bomb on her village and killed several of her innocent family members. As a young adult, feeling ugly and hopeless, she considered suicide. But then she found a New Testament and became a Christian. For the first time in her life, she was able to forgive those who had taken so much from her.

Here are her own words:

Forgiveness made me free from hatred. I still have many scars on my body and severe pain most days but my heart is cleansed.
Napalm is very powerful but faith, forgiveness and love are

much more powerful. We would not have war at all if everyone could learn how to live with true love, hope and forgiveness.[2]

Issue—forgiveness that conquers
During the Holocaust, untold suffering was systematically meted out on many people. The mind-boggling cruelty left survivors with much more than just physical scars. Some people understandably were consumed by anger, hate, and resentment. Many of these people were not able to readjust to life and died within a few years following their liberation. But there were others who did not just survive but thrived. Several studies of these Holocaust survivors showed that, for these victims of the most horrible suffering, forgiveness was the key factor in finding healing and picking up their lives. Without forgiveness, we remain victims.

Marilyn Armour, a professor at the Steve Hicks School of Social Work at the University of Texas at Austin, worked with Holocaust survivors to find out what these survivors had done to make sense of what had happened to them. Armour writes, "The whole idea of forgiveness is an intentional act by the victim. . . . It's not something that just happens."[3] These victims had to forgive—that is, come to the point of being willing to abandon their right to resentment, condemnation, and vengeance toward those who had treated them so cruelly.

Forgiveness is a decision that does not always come easily. It is a spiritual, supernatural exercise and an exercise we will have to undertake over and over again, especially if the hurt has been very deep. We do not forgive because the other person deserves it—he or she does not—but we make the decision to forgive because it is what we have received from God, and we need to pay it forward in order to heal. And strangely, as we practice forgiveness, we catch a glimpse of God's joy and gladness and warmth and character that transform our entire being. We begin to enter His rest.

Worldview—justice will be served

Following World War II, the Allied victors established, in the city of Nuremberg in southern Germany, a court dealing with the atrocities committed by the Nazis. After long years of war, with all the death and suffering, life could not just simply go back to normal. The mass murders committed in extermination camps could not just simply be forgiven and forgotten. The Nuremberg trials were closely followed worldwide as they were seen to provide a platform, however small, for justice against accused Nazi war criminals—many of whom were sentenced to long prison sentences or death.

After the fall of apartheid in South Africa, something new was tried. The newly formed coalition government established the Truth and Reconciliation Commission. The Truth and Reconciliation Commission was court-like. The victims of human rights violations could give statements about their experiences. The perpetrators of these violations could also give testimony and then obtain amnesty from prosecution for their wrongs. In other words, the victims could be heard, but there was no punishment for the perpetrators.

Although this process was revolutionary and has since been used in other countries, the victims of abuse during the apartheid era generally felt that the commission had failed. When the Truth and Reconciliation Commission finished its work, the regular law courts were flooded with victims looking for justice.

Deep down in our hearts, we seem to know that justice is a prerequisite for reconciliation. Someone has to pay for the hurt and pain that evil causes before there can be reconciliation. And this is where life gets complicated. While all of us have been hurt, we have also all caused hurt. Victims often become perpetrators when they have the opportunity. Many child abusers were themselves abused as children.

The only way out of this vicious circle is to look for the ultimate justice. Christians can forgive and leave behind the pain and hurt because Someone has paid the price. "For He made Him who knew no sin to be sin for us, that we might become the righteousness of God in Him" (2 Corinthians 5:21, NKJV). Because Jesus became sin for us, we are free to forgive and be forgiven.

Digging deep—what goes around comes around
Jesus' model prayer can be found in two of the four New Testament Gospels: Matthew 6:9–15 and Luke 11:2–4. Matthew places it within the larger context of the Sermon on the Mount (Matthew 5–7), where Jesus laid out the key principles of His kingdom. Most scholars agree that Matthew, while writing in Greek, addressed a primarily Jewish audience. He is concerned with calling the attention of his readers to the fact that Jesus truly was the fulfillment of Old Testament prophecies. His preference for certain terminology (such as, e.g., "the kingdom of heaven" [Matthew 3:2; 4:17; 5:3; etc.] instead of Luke's preferred "the kingdom of God" [Luke 4:43; 6:20; 7:28; etc.]) reflects the Jewish practice of not using God's name, which, again, points to a Jewish audience. Luke, on the other hand, seems to aim at a Gentile audience and often includes explanations about customs and geography (e.g., Luke 2:22–24; 22:1; 24:13).

Both Gospels contain similar wording of the Lord's Prayer—except for the reference to forgiveness. Matthew 6:12 reads, "And forgive us our *debts*, as we forgive our debtors" (NKJV; emphasis added), while Luke 11:4 says, "And forgive us our *sins*, for we also forgive everyone who is indebted to us" (NKJV; emphasis added). The Greek term *opheilemata*, used by Matthew, means "debt" or "that which is owed in a financial sense" (cf. Romans 4:4). It could also be applied to moral debts: children owe respect and honor to their parents, and parents owe their children love and care. Adventist missiologist Gottfried Oosterwal summarizes this debt as follows: "In Jewish thinking at the time of Christ, the Aramaic term *choba* and its literal translation into Greek, *opheilemata*, implied that all of these obligations, duties, and expectations were considered a debt toward God, for in a life lived *coram Deo*—'before God'—love to God and to our neighbor implies that we fulfill them all. The term *debt*, then, implied a lack of love toward God and our fellow human beings, and therefore was considered sin—an act and sign of a broken relationship between God and us."[4]

In Luke's translation of Jesus' sermon (most likely given in Aramaic), the key word is *hamartia*, "sins" (Luke 11:4). Luke's Gentile audience needed to know that any debt, any obligation, and any unfulfilled promise (be it financial, social, ethical, or moral) should be understood as sin toward God and required divine forgiveness. Interestingly, Luke uses "indebted" in the second half of verse 4—*after* he had established that forgiveness always has a vertical dimension. When we hurt someone, when we cheat someone, or when we speak dismissively of someone in his or her absence, we do not just wrong or fail that person—we fail God because we destroy His image in our neighbor.

Sin is both the "transgression of the law" (1 John 3:4, KJV) and the attitudes and motivations that are often not immediately visible in our actions. Jesus made this point repeatedly in His sermon on the mount. For example, He told His audience that just looking at a woman "lustfully" (Matthew 5:28) means that the person is already guilty of committing adultery. When Jesus carried our sin to the cross, He did not just carry the visible sins (including adultery, murder, theft, and myriads more) but also carried the invisible ones—the attitudes that nobody may be able to see. Jesus knew that God's grace and forgiveness are not optional—only for those who are "really bad sinners." We "all have sinned and fall short of the glory of God," wrote Paul in Romans 3:23. We all need forgiveness and grace every minute of our existence. Praise God that He is compassionate. His compassion is not only seen in Jesus hanging on the cross; rather, His grace has also pursued us throughout the ages. Note this description in Psalm 103:10–13:

He does not deal with us according to our sins,
    nor repay us according to our iniquities.
For as the heavens are high above the earth,
    so great is his steadfast love toward those who fear him;

as far as the east is from the west,
   so far he removes our transgressions from us.
As a father has compassion for his children,
   so the LORD has compassion for those who fear him (NRSV).

Once we have recognized the immense (and continuous) debt-relief program undertaken by our heavenly Father, we are called to pay it forward. We forgive, for we have been forgiven. Forgiveness received but not replicated becomes stale and irrelevant. How can we not forgive those who have hurt us, those who have rejected us, and those who have (perhaps even systematically) humiliated us when our sins— similar in nature but directed at others and at God—have been forgiven and we have been offered clean slates?

Implications—forgiveness is not blind

When we speak of forgiveness, unfortunately, people who are in abusive relationships are often told to forgive their abusers and give them another chance. Tragically, the Bible and religion are often used as a cover for abuse. Abuse will cause the victim to have a distorted concept of God, and the eternal salvation of both victim and abuser are at stake if the abuse is not stopped. We have all been bought through Jesus' blood, and legally we are His. Anyone who is abusive is attacking someone who belongs to Jesus and is, in fact, attacking Him (see Matthew 25:40).

While forgiveness needs to happen for healing to begin, forgiveness does not mean letting an abuser continue his or her abusive patterns.

Biblical forgiveness is not condoning or excusing what someone has done (Isaiah 5:20) or trying to pretend that it did not happen (remember David's sin that is so well documented in 2 Samuel 12). Forgiveness means that we turn our resentment, our hurt, and our desire for revenge over to God (Psalm 37:8, 9). Someone does not even have to ask for forgiveness or be sorry for what he or she has done for us to forgive that person. Forgiveness is not really about the person who has

70

wronged us. It is about stepping out and deciding to move from victim to victor. As someone once described it: not forgiving is like drinking poison while hoping that the other person will die.

Take a breather—God is in the business of grace

"If my people, who are called by my name, will humble themselves and pray and seek my face and turn from their wicked ways, then I will hear from heaven, and I will forgive their sin and will heal their land" (2 Chronicles 7:14). This text describes God's answer to Solomon's dedicatory prayer during the inauguration of the temple. God, who calls His people by His own name, lists four qualities that precede His forgiveness and that will result in the healing of the land. We first need to humble ourselves; we need to recognize our true condition. Then we pray to the only One capable of saving us. This prayer expresses two attitudes: we yearn to see His face, not His back, and then we turn from what will ultimately destroy us.

> *Who is a God like you,*
> *who pardons sin and forgives the transgression*
> *of the remnant of his inheritance?*
> *You do not stay angry forever*
> *but delight to show mercy (Micah 7:18).*

People worshiped many different gods in Old Testament times, but YHWH was unique. Micah's initial question is actually somewhat of a tongue-in-cheek question, for Micah's name meant: "Who is like the Lord?" Micah knew without a doubt that God was different, for He forgives sins. He also knew that God's anger was primarily directed at sin and that He delighted to show His compassion to the sinner. What would happen if we could emulate this delight in forgiving others freely and unreservedly?

"You, Lord, are forgiving and good, abounding in love to all who call to you" (Psalm 86:5). Like so many other Old Testament texts, this

text is anchored in the best description (and the most quoted by later biblical authors) of God's character found in Exodus 34:6, 7. God's goodness and His abounding love (or compassionate love) drive His willingness to forgive. If we could just grasp how invested in this world He is!

"Be kind and compassionate to one another, forgiving each other, just as in Christ God forgave you" (Ephesians 4:32). Forgiveness illustrates our kindness and compassion and is anchored in God's forgiveness. New Testament scholar Andrew Lincoln put it this way: "What God has done in Christ for believers, which has been the theme of the first half of the letter [to the Ephesians], now provides both the norm and the grounds for believers' own behavior. God's forgiveness of them becomes the paradigm for their mutual forgiveness."[5]

---

1. Ian K. Smith, "South Vietnam, 9 June 1972 | Nick Ut," *New Statesman*, April 1, 2010, https://www.newstatesman.com/culture/2010/03/nick-ut-vietnamese-girl.

2. Kim Phuc, "The Long Road to Forgiveness," NPR, June 30, 2008, https://www.npr.org/templates/story/story.php?storyId=91964687.

3. "Holocaust Survivors' Testimonials Shed Light on Our Ability to Recover After Traumatic Experiences, Researcher Finds," UT News, April 20, 2009, https://news.utexas.edu/2009/04/20/holocaust-survivors-testimonials-shed-light-on-our-ability-to-recover-after-traumatic-experiences-researcher-finds/. For more about this research project, see Marilyn Armour and Roberta R. Greene, Holocaust Survivors: A Study in Resilience," *Journal of Gerontological Social Work* 37.1 (2002): 3-18, https://www.academia.edu/5943995/Holocaust_Survivors_A_Study_in_Resilience.

4. Gottfried Oosterwal, *The Lord's Prayer Through Primitive Eyes: A Stone Age People's Journey* (Nampa, ID: Pacific Press®, 2009), 124.

5. Andrew T. Lincoln, *Ephesians*, Word Biblical Commentary, vol. 42 (Dallas, TX: Word, 1990), 310.

Eight

Free to Rest

A while ago a short video clip made the rounds on social media. In it, a young woman works with her gray-haired father in the kitchen. As they cook together, the woman asks her father whether he liked the new iPad she had bought him for Christmas. The father nods but does not seem overly excited.

She asks whether he managed with the setup and apps. He looks at her blankly. There is a moment's silence, and then he assures her that it was a very nice gift. The camera then pans out, and we see him scrape a chopped tomato into a dish and then rinse and put into the dishwasher the iPad that he obviously thought was a chopping board.

Sometimes we do not appreciate what we have been given. We often do not realize how wonderful something is until we lose it. This is probably the truest with our health. We often take our intricately designed bodies for granted until the moment we get sick.

Issue—far from healthy
Even though we enjoy better health care and more cures for diseases than ever before, we are far from being healthy. What has changed over the years, however, are the kinds of diseases that afflict us.

Smallpox, bubonic plague, and tuberculosis, which accounted for a large number of deaths, now have vaccines or treatments. With the dawn of the twentieth century and the explosion of knowledge in the health sciences, many predicted an end to disease by the conclusion of the century.

Unfortunately, while some cures have been discovered, many more diseases have emerged. Rather than looking to pills and medication, we are discovering that health is much more than just the absence of disease. The top diseases claiming the most lives in the developed world include heart disease, cancer, and diabetes, which are often associated with lifestyle.[1]

Not all diseases of epidemic proportions have visible symptoms. One that is often not spoken about in Christian circles is depression. Depression, according to the World Health Organization, is the leading cause of disability worldwide and is a major contributor to the global burden of disease.[2] Depression is that nameless something that drains our joy, takes our rest, and robs us of hope. Depression can be due to genetics or can be caused by an emotional trigger, such as the death of someone close. It can also just gradually settle over us as a reaction to living in a stressful world. As depression sets in, we often turn to coping mechanisms that prove to be self-destructive. We may start taking sleeping tablets to try to get some rest and then discover that we cannot sleep without them, or we may begin to overeat or bury ourselves in work to try to escape. When we realize that, instead of helping, we have dug ourselves into a deeper hole, and guilt comes crushing in on us.

Depression has a way of sucking us into a dark whirlpool of self-loathing. And sometimes we begin to think that death is the only way out. The good news is that God understands better than we do what we are up against as we fight depression. God knows that more than the physical tiredness that comes with depression, we are emotionally tired and carry a tremendous load of guilt.

God wants to free us from this load of guilt and give us rest. This is not a one-time event or cure. Entering into God's rest has to do with healing—with slowly unlearning negative thought patterns and destructive habits. We may need professional help to guide us in this process. God understands that life in this sinful world can and will cause emotional pain and sometimes even depression, but instead of letting it drive us away from Him, He invites us to run into His arms.

Worldview—who is guilty?
Most ancient civilizations connected sickness to the supernatural. Sick people were often seen as demon possessed or had some curse on them. There was little to no understanding of the conditions that fostered disease and, of course, no understanding of bacteria, viruses, or genetically caused diseases or the natural laws that help to maintain health. All disease was seen as either a curse from God (or the gods) or the result of the direct intervention of Satan or evil spirits.

This worldview, present in both Jewish and pagan cultures, is brought into focus in the story, found in John 9, involving a man born blind. Jesus' disciples ask the crucial question that was on the minds of many: "Rabbi, who sinned, this man or his parents, that he was born blind?" (verse 2, NKJV). The question reflected the popular assumption that every illness could be directly traced back to a specific sin and that someone or something was responsible for the condition. Jesus strongly rejects this worldview in verse 3 by stating that neither the man himself nor his parents were responsible for the blindness. In other words, the blindness could not be pinned on a particular sin of the man or his parents. This must have been a radically new thought for the disciples. Finding out who is to blame does not bring healing or wholeness.

Jesus turns the disciples' thoughts away from trying to find out *who* was to blame by pointing out that even this very negative situation could be used by God to demonstrate His power to bring relief and healing (verse 3).

The biblical worldview involving sin and disease is more nuanced and reflects a more complicated reality than the direct cause and effect people believed in. Before sin, there was no sickness. With sin came the entrance of all that hurts, destroys, and eventually kills. God's original design did not include pain, disease, and suffering. But as long as we are in this sin-sick world, there will be no guarantees on health.

Even though disease was used as a punishment on occasion (e.g., Numbers 16), and even though demons did and do possess people (e.g., Matthew 4:24), most diseases are not directly caused by God or Satan. As individuals, God has given us choices. That is why God gives us health guidelines and advice so that we can enjoy a better quality of life. While some of an individual's health is influenced by things beyond his or her control (diseases based on genetics, such as sickle cell disease), there are also natural health laws that God has revealed in His Word. The good news is that when we find ourselves sick as a result of our own doing, from someone else's neglect, or just as a by-product of living in this sinful world, God still wants to give us rest and draw us to Him.

Digging deep—the power of *shalom*
Scientists tell us that health is a complex interplay of body systems, involving mental and emotional components. Health is more than the absence of disease. At least, that is the impression one gets when looking at the portrayal of healthy people in Scripture. The Bible, as noted by John Wilkinson, "presents its teaching [about health] not by definition and argument, but by illustration and example. It lays before its readers not a definition of health systematically expounded, but a picture of the characteristics of healthy people as seen in their life, their character and their actions."[3] The focus in many of the Bible's stories is on well-being, righteousness, obedience, strength, fertility, and longevity. For example, a godly person, such as Abraham, is considered righteous, faithful, and obedient (Genesis 15:6). Consequently, there is the promise of well-being (or *shalom*), rest, and long life (verse 15).

The holistic perspective on health as the result of many interrelated elements—some of which have no apparent physiological links—is distinct from traditional Western thought and philosophy. In order to grasp this better, we will discuss in more detail the nature of *shalom*, "peace, well-being,"[4] and then focus on the priestly blessing found in Numbers 6:24–26 that culminates in the divine promise of finding *shalom*.

The root *shalom* appears in most Semitic languages, including Hebrew and Aramaic. It communicates totality and completeness. The noun appears more than 230 times in the Old Testament in many varied contexts. It can describe harmony and peace between individuals or groups (e.g., Genesis 26:31) as well as tribes and nations (e.g., Judges 4:17; 1 Samuel 7:14). Some texts link *prosperity* with *shalom*, especially in the context of the wicked (e.g., Job 15:21; Psalm 73:3); ultimately, there is no true *shalom* for the wicked since they have disconnected themselves from God, who is the true Source of *shalom* (Isaiah 48:22; 57:21).

A normal greeting in Old Testament times was, "*Shalom* to you," often translated as a question—"Are you well?" (e.g., Genesis 29:6; 43:27; 2 Samuel 18:29). If someone did not feel well, he would say that he had no *shalom* in his bones (Psalm 38:3). This brief overview clearly illustrates the challenge Bible translators face with the word *shalom* because the term denotes something that is far more comprehensive than the way we use the words *health* and *peace*. Shalom, or true well-being, is a God-given gift.

Numbers 6:24–26 contains the wording of the blessings Aaron and his sons were to pronounce over Israel.

"The LORD bless you and keep you;
The LORD make His face shine upon you,
And be gracious to you;
The LORD lift up His countenance upon you,
And give you peace [*shalom*]" (NKJV).

This blessing, written in Hebrew poetry, points toward the culmination of God giving *shalom* to His people. Such spoken blessings are not independent magic words but emanate from Israel's Creator and Savior. Only God can make them become a reality. They do not carry in themselves any magical agency or significance.

Blessing in this context means living under the protection and shelter of the Lord. This protection from harm can involve human agents (Isaiah 31:5) or demonic forces (Psalm 121:3, 4, 7). To be blessed means to be safe. Causing one's face to shine upon someone expresses favor, pleasure, and benevolence. If this principle is applied to the text, the blessing means that the Lord will be gracious to the one upon whom the blessing has been pronounced. Finally, when God "lifts up His countenance" upon somebody, this will result in *shalom*, "peace." God's *shalom* encompasses and affects all areas of human existence. We become whole—even in the face of death, disease, and disappointment.

Intriguingly, according to Numbers 6:27, pronouncing a priestly blessing on "the children of Israel" (NKJV) results in marking individuals (the blessings were expressed in singular verbal forms) as belonging to God. The priests were to literally "put My name on the children of Israel" (verse 27, NKJV). The Lord is right at the center of the blessing. He *is* Israel's source of blessing, and when the blessing is pronounced, it marks those receiving the blessing as His property. This concept of belonging lies at the center of *shalom*. We can rest in our Creator and Savior because we know that we are His. And when we belong to Him, we will experience *shalom*. This does not necessarily suggest the absence of disease. Rather, it points us to our greater need. We need to belong and find safety in the arms of our caring heavenly Father.

Implications—I am your Healer
If God really is the Source of *shalom* for this world and for each of us personally, and He knows how we were "knit . . . together" in our

mother's womb (Psalm 139:13), He must also be our Healer as suggested in Exodus 15:26. Does this mean that when we are faced with disease and illness, we just have to pray and ask God for healing?

Some Christians seem to believe this, and healing ministries often form an important element of charismatic worship. Undoubtedly, prayer is an important part of finding the sense of well-being that God promises His children. At times, God uses miracles to heal the sick. But the Creator God also established laws, including health laws, that help us to live "whole" lives. In fact, many of the Levitical laws, which addressed public-health issues involving the appropriate diet (including also the laws found in Leviticus 11 concerning clean meat), clean water, the disposal of sewage, burial of the dead, sexuality, as well as quarantine legislation affecting those with communicable diseases, provided by God as part of His covenant with Israel, had a direct impact on public and personal health.[5]

This balance between prevention and healing is part of the DNA of the Adventist health message. As noted on the website of the General Conference of Seventh-day Adventists Health Ministries Department:

We believe in a "ministry of healing" by which people can be restored to wholeness. Reflecting on the life of Christ, the apostle Luke wrote that "Jesus increased in wisdom, in stature, and in favor with God and man" (Luke 2:52). Here we see the four dimensions of wholistic health: mental, physical, spiritual, and social. We believe in "whole-person care," which addresses each of these dimensions.

We emphasize the prevention of disease and relief of suffering through simple lifestyle habits that correspond with the way God created us to live, and at the same time acknowledge the effectiveness of evidence-based therapy when disease has already occurred.[6]

Since God is the Author of true science and established this incredible web of natural laws that govern the universe, evidence-based, high-quality research is part of God's plan to bring healing to a hurting world. That is why the Seventh-day Adventist Church operates a large network of hospitals and clinics around the world, often associated with research facilities and medical schools. God wants us to be His healing hands—through prevention as well as quality health care.

Take a breather—take Him at His word

"He heals the brokenhearted and binds up their wounds" (Psalm 147:3). God's care for us includes our broken hearts and wounded souls. This is a psalm that we should read in dark moments, for it celebrates God's provision and care. We can take Him at His word.

" *'He himself bore our sins' in his body on the cross, so that we might die to sins and live for righteousness; 'by his wounds you have been healed' "* *(1 Peter 2:24).* Peter is quoting intermittently from Isaiah 52:12–53:12, highlighting Christ's example of submission. We receive restoration and healing because He carried our sins and offers us new life.

"Behold, I will bring . . . health and healing; I will heal them and reveal to them the abundance of peace and truth" (Jeremiah 33:6, NKJV). This is part of a prophetic vision of God's people following their return from Babylonian exile. Healing and health are part of God's plan for those who choose to follow Him wholeheartedly.

---

1. "What Are the Top 50 Deadly and Widespread Diseases?," FactDr, last updated October 11, 2019, https://factdr.com/uncategorized/top-50-deadly-diseases/.

2. "Depression," World Health Organization, January 30, 2020, http://www.who.int/news-room/fact-sheets/detail/depression.

3. John Wilkinson, *The Bible and Healing: A Medical and Theological Commentary* (Grand Rapids, MI: Eerdmans, 1998), 11.

4. This is based on Wilkinson, 11–13, who offers more details and additional references.

5. For specific biblical examples, see George W. Reid, "Health and Healing," in *Handbook of Seventh-day Adventist Theology*, ed. Raoul Dederen (Hagerstown, MD: Review and Herald®, 2000), 772–776.

6. "Who We Are: Philosophy," Adventist Health Ministries, accessed October 29, 2020, https://www.healthministries.com/philosophy.

Nine

The Rhythms of Rest

It must have been something to watch light break through the darkness and silent oceans explode with squirming aquatic life of every sort, see the first bird take flight, and watch Adam take his first breath. It must have been wonderful. But then, after all of this active creating, God turned His attention to something else. At first glance, it did not seem as spectacular as breaching whales or dazzling feather displays; God just simply made a day—the seventh day—and made it special. God created *Shabbat*, a day of rest. Even before humanity dashed off on our self-imposed stressful lives, God established a marker—a living memory aid. This day would be a time to stop and deliberately enjoy life. A day to be and not do; a day to celebrate the gift of grass, air, wildlife, water, people, and most of all, the Creator of every good gift. This was no one-time invitation that expired with the exile from Eden. God wanted to make sure that the invitation could stand the test of time, and so right from the beginning, He knitted it into the very fabric of time. There would always be the invitation to a restful celebration of Creation, again and again and again, with every seventh day.

Issue—equal freedom

Slavery was hard. Every day was like the day before and filled with mind-numbing physical labor. The Israelites needed rest badly. God heard, God saw, and God gave rest. With one of the most dramatic exits in history, God saved His people from slavery in Egypt (Exodus 12) and retaught them about His wonderful gift of rest. One of the first lessons the former slaves learned was that God's rest is the great equalizer and restorer of relationships. God's freedom did not mean a simple inversion of the status quo where former slaves became the new masters. Now that they were free, they were not free to exert their freedom at the expense of others (Deuteronomy 15:12–18, esp. verse 15).

The Sabbath rest that God had in mind was a time to let the donkey sleep in (cf. Exodus 20:10). While the ox contentedly chewed its cud, parents would have time to watch cloud formations with their arms tucked around their children. Dozing servants could sit in the shade. And even the foreigner could rest secure in the knowledge that he was not excluded because of where he came from or how he looked; he had a right to God's celebration of rest too. The Israelites were invited every seventh day to observe a festival of freedom. Every Sabbath they were to remember who they had been (slaves) and who they now were (God's children)—a part of creation and a part of a new nation that God was taking home (Deuteronomy 5:15).

Worldview—all or nothing

Evolution has become one of the most widespread, basic worldviews. The theory holds that all life evolved by a series of natural processes in nature. Under the influence of this worldview, many Christians have attempted to bring evolutionary theory and biblical origins together in their worldviews. The concept of theistic evolution is one of these attempts to bring together what seems diametrically opposed. Theistic evolution suggests that God created the building blocks of life but then withdrew and allowed nature to take its course and progress in an evolutionary way.

Theistic evolution creates more problems than it solves. It clearly undermines the biblical worldview that starts with "In the beginning God created . . ." (Genesis 1:1). The seventh-day Sabbath brings theistic evolution into sharp contrast with the biblical account, which has God creating the earth in six literal twenty-four-hour days, with the seventh day being a memorial to this Creation event.

Believing in theistic evolution undermines our belief in a personal, loving God who is involved in history as a whole and also in our personal history. Theistic evolution, with its long time periods, also raises concerns about death. The Bible describes death as the result of the entrance of sin. Theistic evolution has God permitting death for millions of years, with whole species evolving and becoming extinct before the evolution of man. In effect, this theory sees God use death as part of the "creation" process, which is contradictory to the entire biblical record, where death is described as the enemy and the consequence of the entrance of sin.

If death is somehow part of God's creative plan, then why would Jesus need to come to save us from sin that leads to death? Moving away from a literal reading of our origins also leads to questioning other biblical truths, such as the Second Coming or the resurrection of the dead. The weekly Sabbath celebration is a reminder that "He is God; it is He who has made us, and not we ourselves; we are His people and the sheep of His pasture" (Psalm 100:3, NKJV).

Digging deep—between creation and liberation
Creation is one of the most foundational theological themes in the Bible. Both testaments contain hundreds of direct intertextual links, allusions, and echoes that remind the reader that God's creative activity was taken as a given by all biblical authors.[1] God as the Creator is the foundation of any Old Testament theology. As noted by Old Testament scholar Rolf Rendtorff: "The . . . authors of the Hebrew Bible understood creation not as *one* topic among others or even one of lower significance. For them creation was the starting point, because everything human beings can think and say about God and his relation to

the world and to humankind depends on the fact that he created all this."[2]

God's creation was "very good" (Genesis 1:31), and it included the creation of time. Creation was complete only with the installation of the Sabbath on the seventh day. On this day, "God ended His work which He had done, and He rested on the seventh day from all His work which He had done" (Genesis 2:2, NKJV). The Sabbath is the ultimate culmination of Creation, for it provides both time and space for community and holiness. God's rest becomes the paradigm for our Sabbath rest. God does not rest because He is tired (cf. Isaiah 40:28) but because He models community with His creation. No other day in the Creation account is "blessed" and "sanctified" by God (Genesis 2:3, NKJV). Like all creation, the Sabbath belongs to Him, and when we rest, we confirm our commitment to also belong to Him.

Following the foundational stories of Creation and the Fall in Genesis 1–3, the references to the Sabbath in the Pentateuch—the Torah, or Law—appear in both narrative and legal contexts. We will review two narratives relating to the Sabbath in the Pentateuch and then focus on the Sabbath command in the Ten Commandments as found in Exodus and Deuteronomy. Finally, we will look at one example of how later prophets referenced Creation and linked it to God's new creation.

The first narrative involving the Sabbath can be found in Exodus 16. It describes how God fed His people with manna—bread from heaven. This heavenly bread sustained Israel during their wilderness journey and was only given on six days. Normally, it would spoil when stored—except on Fridays, when the Israelites would receive a double portion that was sufficient for Friday and Sabbath (Exodus 16:22–30). Israel had to completely rely on God for their physical needs and trust that their Creator would sustain them every Sabbath—even without collecting food. Sabbath rest here is closely linked to faith.

In Numbers 15:32–36, an anonymous Israelite is found gathering "sticks" (NKJV) on the Sabbath day, and following a direct intervention from the Lord in response to a question raised by Moses, is executed by stoning outside the camp. The exact nature of the man's activity is described using a form of the verb *qashash*, which only appears eight times in the Old Testament (Exodus 5:7, 12; Numbers 15:32, 33; 1 Kings 17:10, 12; Zephaniah 2:1 [twice]). The prior use of the verb in Exodus 5:7, 12 is of particular interest, as it describes the Israelites' gathering of stubble for the production of bricks in response to increased Egyptian oppression.[3] Old Testament scholar Mathilde Frey argues that the use of this particular verb suggests "that the Israelite man, even though freed from slavery, consciously chose to act against the law of freedom and thereby placed himself back into the position of a slave."[4] Liberation and Creation rest need to be considered together and remind us of the two complementary motive clauses of the Sabbath commandment in Exodus 20:8–11 and Deuteronomy 5:12–15.

The initial "remember" at the outset of the Sabbath commandment in Exodus 20:8 already points us back to Creation. We can only remember what we already know. This strongly suggests that the Sabbath was not a new institution established at Mount Sinai. Verse 11 offers the rationale for resting and keeping the Sabbath holy: "For in six days the LORD made the heavens and the earth, the sea, and all that is in them, and rested the seventh day" (NKJV). Israel had a history, and it began with God's creative action. The biblical text refers back to a time *before* the misery of slavery became Israel's reality. God's Sabbath was part of this history. In fact, this history goes right back to the beginning. The Sabbath commandment anchors Israel in Creation.

Deuteronomy 5:12–15 uses a different rationale. It starts off with "observe," reminding a new generation standing at the border of the Promised Land that they needed to guard and protect the boundaries of sacred Sabbath time. Once we have *remembered*, we need to *guard* and *observe* God's special gift of rest. Verse 15 offers another rationale for guarding the Sabbath: "And remember that you were a slave in the land of Egypt, and the LORD your God brought you out from there by a mighty hand and by an outstretched arm" (NKJV). God was not only the Creator but also Israel's Liberator, or to use New Testament terminology, their Savior. These two rationales are not contradictory. Israel's liberation from slavery was, in fact, an implicit reference to a "new" creation, harking back to God's original Creation. Furthermore, a people perched on the edge of the Promised Land needed to remember God's saving acts—"by a mighty hand and by an outstretched arm"—for this image of their unlikely liberation by an almighty God sustained them as they faced seemingly never-ending challenges of powerful military alliances, fortified city-states, and often, their own lack of faith. Each Sabbath reminded them of their Creator and their Redeemer. God's weekly rhythm of rest is a reminder of our origin and our status. We were lovingly created and liberated from the power of (sin's) slavery.

Jeremiah 4:23–26 offers a glimpse into how Israel's prophets often referenced Creation in their visions of Israel's future. This section contains "strong linguistic markers to the creation account as found in Genesis 1. The oracle of doom presents possibly the most faithful account of de-creation, or the reversal of creation, when compared to Genesis 1:2–2:4a."[5] Jeremiah follows the sequence of the days of Creation as he describes the reversal of Creation. "While the Genesis account ends with [a] day of rest, the Sabbath, Jeremiah's de-creation account ends with a day of fury ["at the presence of the LORD, by His fierce anger" (Jeremiah 4:26, NKJV)]. The deconstruction of creation is taking place, and one can be sure that the listeners (and subsequent readers) of the prophet's message recognized the creation pattern. Creation becomes the paradigm for destruction and serves as the primeval point of departure for" Jeremiah's inspired contextualization of the coming judgment.[6]

Implications—taking care of God's business
Some Christians, especially Seventh-day Adventists, feel some reluctance about being involved in any environmental programs aimed at "saving"

the planet because these are often attached to political agendas. Others state that there is no point in trying to save the planet because prophecy foretells that things will disintegrate anyway, and the earth will be destroyed by fire, and a new heaven and new earth will be created by God. This kind of reasoning ignores the essential role of stewardship to which we are called. Stewardship is an important consequence of Creation, and the weekly Sabbath reminds us of that stewardship. Genesis 1 mentions twice the task of having "dominion" over the creatures (verses 26, 28, NKJV). Adam and Eve, having been created in God's image and according to His likeness, were to echo God's loving and caring dominion over creation. As God's stewards, they were not called to exploit but to care. Being created in God's image enabled humanity to distinguish between exploitation and stewardship. Stewardship acknowledges God as the Owner of all goods (Psalm 24:1, 2) and the Source of all power (Deuteronomy 8:18). Biblical stewardship involves service (Matthew 20:25–28) and accountability (Matthew 25:14–30).

The seventh-day Sabbath functions as a weekly reminder that we are part of God's team, serving His creation. Stewardship does not have to be connected to political agendas but has practical consequences for our personal choices. As we make lifestyle choices in order to care for our bodies as best we can, even with the challenges of the genes we have inherited and the inevitability of old age, so, too, can we make choices about how we look after the environment by consciously choosing products and services that have as little negative impact on the environment as possible. We can also oppose cruelty to animals by our dietary choices. Even though our natural world is a far cry from Eden's beauty, we can continue to celebrate the beauty and wonder of creation as we anticipate the new creation when God will finally restore our world to its Edenic glory.

Take a breather—moments of rest
God's rhythm of rest is not limited to the seventh-day Sabbath rest.

While we need the weekly reminder of who we are and what God wants us to be, we also need to find daily moments of spiritual refreshment. Jesus' example may offer the best paradigm.

"Now in the morning, having risen a long while before daylight, He [Jesus] went out and departed to a solitary place; and there He prayed" *(Mark 1:35, NKJV).* Jesus, the God-man, needed to commune daily with His heavenly Father. Getting up while it was still dark, He searched for a quiet place and spent time in conversation with the Father. Communion with God was His key to a life of service that extended grace to all. "In a life wholly devoted to the good of others," writes Ellen White,

> the Saviour found it necessary to withdraw from the thorough-fares of travel and from the throng that followed Him day after day. He must turn aside from a life of ceaseless activity and contact with human needs, to seek retirement and unbroken communion with His Father. As one with us, a sharer in our needs and weaknesses, He was wholly dependent upon God, and in the secret place of prayer He sought divine strength, that He might go forth braced for duty and trial. In a world of sin Jesus endured struggles and torture of soul. In communion with God He could unburden the sorrows that were crushing Him. Here He found comfort and joy.[7]

---

1. See, e.g., the numerous examples found in *"He Spoke and It Was": Divine Creation in the Old Testament*, ed. Gerald A. Klingbeil, Creation Series, vol. 1 (Nampa, ID: Pacific Press®, 2015). A forthcoming volume dealing with the use of the Creation motif in the New Testament is currently being edited by Tom Shepherd.

2. Rolf Rendtorff, "Some Reflections on Creation as a Topic of Old Testament Theology," in *Priests, Prophets and Scribes: Essays on the Formation and Heritage of Second Temple Judaism in Honour of Joseph Blenkinsopp*, ed. Eugene Ulrich, John W. Wright, Robert P. Carroll, and Philip R. Davies, *Journal for the Study of the Old Testament*, Supplement Series 149 (Sheffield, UK: Sheffield Academic Press, 1992), 207; emphasis added.

3. Tzvi Novick, "Law and Loss: Response to Catastrophe in Numbers 15," *Harvard Theo-*

logical Review 101, no. 1 (January 2008): 5; for more detail, see Mathilde Frey, "The Wood-gatherer's Sabbath: A Literary Study of Numbers 15:32–36," *Journal of Asia Adventist Seminary* 13, no. 1 (2010): 6.

4. Frey, 6. A similar conclusion is found in Jonathan Burnside, " 'What Shall We Do With the Sabbath-Gatherer?' A Narrative Approach to a 'Hard Case' in Biblical Law (Numbers 15:32–36)," *Vetus Testamentum* 60, no. 1 (2010): 45–62.

5. Martin G. Klingbeil, "Creation in the Prophetic Literature of the Old Testament: An Intertextual Approach," in *The Genesis Creation Account and Its Reverberations in the Old Testament*, ed. Gerald A. Klingbeil (Berrien Springs, MI: Andrews University Press, 2015), 279; see also Klingbeil, 257–289.

6. Klingbeil, 279.

7. Ellen G. White, *The Desire of Ages* (Mountain View, CA: Pacific Press®, 1940), 362, 363.

Ten

Sabbath Rest

A group of parents, clergy, and community leaders met in Ridgewood, New Jersey, to discuss a pressing problem. They had all noticed and experienced life becoming too hectic and joyless. Garland Allen, the director of wellness for schools in Ridgewood, voiced the concerns of many when he said, "We're creating a generation that's overscheduled by parents, overtested by teachers and overtrained by coaches."

In response to this, the group developed the first Ready, Set, Relax! project for March 26, 2002. The concept was simple. On that day, schools would not assign any homework. Clubs would not schedule meetings, and sports teams would cancel practice. Parents would come home from work and take time with their families.[1] Everyone thought that the idea was great, and the first day of the project seemed to be appreciated by those who took part. It drew nationwide media attention, and several other towns also tried it, but after a few years, it seemed to fizzle out.[2]

It seems that as much as we all realize that we need this time-out, actually taking it is difficult—we just cannot let go. In a world where we cannot let go, a command to stop can be a tremendous blessing.

Issue—Sabbath and holiness

A careful reading of the two complementary Creation reports found in Genesis 1 and 2 highlights one important fact: God only deemed the seventh day—the Sabbath—as holy. The earth, space, stars and luminaries, land, plants, sea, animals, and even human beings are never designated as *qadash*, "holy" (Genesis 2:3). Other cultures and religions treasure holy mountains or holy springs, even holy trees. But God declares time holy, for it is God's blessing and His presence that transform a regular twenty-four-hour day into a temple of time that diffuses holiness.

Holiness in the Old Testament is closely associated with God. His presence transforms something mundane into something holy. A burning bush, not consumed by the fire, becomes "holy ground" (Exodus 3:5) when God speaks out of the fire and calls Moses to lead His people from the "house of slavery" into the Promised Land. People become holy when they are consecrated to the Lord (the Hebrew uses a causative verbal form of *qadash*, "to make holy"), as happens during the ordination ritual of Aaron and his sons in Leviticus 8:30.

Scripture's first reference to holiness focuses on time. "Adam and Eve were invited to 'keep' that seventh day holy," writes Christian author A. J. Swoboda. "Do not misread the text: they were not to *make* the Sabbath holy. Humans cannot make anything holy."[3] God declaring the seventh-day Sabbath holy makes a statement that resonates through time and space. This time is not empty or devoid of something. It is full of goodness—and holiness—for God is present. "God established his love-relationship with humanity on the Sabbath and commenced his history in direct relation to the history of the world. God purposefully placed himself face to face with human life and made himself accessible to it, which indicates his intimate interest in his creatures."[4]

While the entrance of sin disrupted the direct access between God and Adam and Eve, Sabbath time spent in conversation with the Creator offered a weekly opportunity to connect, again and again, to the Holy One of Israel. God's holiness, as preserved in the Sabbath, is not just a leftover of Creation; it fills the void created by constant activities and work and helps us to anticipate a new creation.

Worldview—never forget

"Remember" is a unique way to begin a command. None of the other Ten Commandments begin in this way. "Remember" presupposes that there is something to remember—a shared history. In Exodus 20:8–11, the Sabbath command, "Remember the Sabbath day, to keep it holy" (NKJV), takes us straight back to Creation week and helps us remember where we come from. There are also other things that we are called to remember. The Sabbath reminds us that we do not belong to ourselves; we are not independent entities (Genesis 1:26). We were created to live in communities. We remember that marriage and family are key parts of our social fabric and need to be guarded and carefully nurtured.

The repetition of the Sabbath command in Deuteronomy 5:12–15 highlights other things to remember. We not only remember that we are created but also remember that we are free. Sabbath is a celebration of freedom—freedom from sin, freedom from our own attempts at righteousness, and freedom from Egypt and all the things and places that keep us in bondage.

Although we are free, we are still called to remember what it is like to be slaves. The Sabbath is a conscious turning away from our small realities to look at others in faraway places and next door. This remembering to look can be painful as we see the hurting and marginalized. The Sabbath helps us not to grow callous in this world of natural disasters and man-made tragedies, but rather to keep spending ourselves "in behalf of the hungry and satisfy the needs of the oppressed" (Isaiah 58:10). The Sabbath helps us remember that no matter how different we seem and how "foreign" someone may appear to us, God sees us all as His by creation and redemption. Racial, ethnic, socioeconomic, and gender differences are irrelevant. In the New Testament's language, it sounds like this: "There is neither Jew nor Greek, there is neither slave nor free, there is neither male nor female; for you are all one in Christ Jesus" (Galatians 3:28, NKJV). God tells us that resting and relating to our Creator and Redeemer will automatically drive us to look at the rest of creation with different eyes.

Digging deep—understanding God's signage

Signs give us directions. They also alert us to unexpected changes, such as an arrow warning us that a two-lane street will soon turn into a one-lane street due to some street construction. Street signs help us orient ourselves and find our way, especially when we have no cell phone coverage. Signs are points of reference designed to communicate important ideas or concepts.

The Sabbath is more than a reminder that we have been created and saved. The Bible tells us that the Sabbath also "is a sign between Me and you throughout your generations, that you may know that I am the Lord who sanctifies you" (Exodus 31:13, NKJV).

Based on the biblical data, Sabbath keeping is not an optional recreational activity. Rather, it is a divine command by the One who made us and knows how we tick. It also functions as a sign between God and His people and helps us to think biblically about sanctification. Scholars have long recognized the close link between the Sabbath and the sanctuary. Both emphasize divine-human fellowship and community— in space and time (cf. Exodus 25:8). Both were given by God and reflect divine characteristics.

The Sabbath is a sign of a perpetual (or eternal) covenant (Exodus 31:16, 17) rooted in Creation. Scripture mentions three covenant signs in the Old Testament: the rainbow in Genesis 9:12, 13, 17; the circumcision of all male children in Genesis 17:11; and the Sabbath in Exodus 31:13, 17 and Ezekiel 20:12, 20. Of these three, the Sabbath is the least physically tangible and involves a consistent human response. We can easily see rainbows in the sky following a storm. Circumcision is a visible physical sign, but it is the Sabbath sign that helps us to know the

Creator, Redeemer, and Sanctifier. Each Sabbath is like a flag that gets raised every seven days and functions as a mnemonic device, for we tend to forget.

It is intriguing that Exodus 31:13 tells us that the Sabbath is the sign that God sanctifies us. The literal translation of this phrase in verse 13 is, "So that I, the Lord, sanctify you." The verbal form of *qadash* refers to holiness. The "you" in the text is a plural form and not a reference to an individual but to a larger community—God's people. We do not become holy when we keep the Sabbath. Rather, we publicly recognize God as our Creator, our Redeemer (especially in the context of the Exodus), and our Sanctifier. Holiness is not based on personal effort but rather on divine action.

Adventists have always recognized the message of the first angel of Revelation 14:6, 7 as pointing to the Sabbath. The language of the text clearly echoes the language of the fourth commandment (cf. Exodus 20:11). In a sense, the Sabbath becomes the subtext of God's story, set in contrast to the dragon's story in Revelation. A loving Creator is set against the angry accuser who wants to sow doubt about the character of God. In the first angel's message, "The Sabbath," writes New Testament scholar Sigve Tonstad, "conveys the message of God's enduring and faithful participation in human reality."[5] God is still around, and every new Sabbath becomes a sign of His presence, grace, and future.

The message of the first "angel flying" in midair is described as "the everlasting gospel" (Revelation 14:6, NKJV) that needs to reach everyone living on Earth. It is God's final effort to offer a credible alternative to Satan's caricature of God and His character; the Sabbath, established at the end of Creation week, becomes the sign of our allegiance to God. Faced with two systems of worship—righteousness by works versus righteousness by faith—we choose to worship the Creator whom we know calls us back to true worship. Keeping the Sabbath holy is a public demonstration that we commit to the One who yearns to spend eternity with His children from every nation, tribe, tongue, and people, just as

He yearned to spend time with Adam and Eve on that first Sabbath in Eden.

Implications—beyond lists

To swim or wade? What about long, sweaty hikes? Is running a soup kitchen downtown a good Sabbath activity? While Sabbath keeping is a key part of our faith, questions of how to properly observe it are often asked. We know that God does not want empty worship or pious silence. He wants to see His people engaged with those surrounding them, especially the downtrodden and marginalized. True Sabbath keeping cannot be a self-centered pursuit of "holiness" by withdrawing from all others and trying to keep from worldly contamination. We know that keeping the Sabbath holy must be more than attending a church service and then living as on any weekday for the rest of the day. But here is the question: How do we keep the Sabbath holy without making a list of rules that can turn our focus to dos and don'ts but, like the Pharisees of Jesus' time, end up missing the "Lord of the Sabbath" (Matthew 12:8)? How can we avoid the trap of drawing up arbitrary lists of appropriate Sabbath activities? The answer lies in understanding the Scripture precepts that help us see beyond rules to the universal, timeless principles that can be applied to all cultures and in all circumstances.

Here is a summary of these biblical principles.

Guiding principles for Sabbath observance

The following are based on God's character and provide a foundation for Sabbath practices:

Preparing for this day to enjoy its benefits.

Resting from work, life's burdens, and secular concerns and distractions.

Renewing: observing the day in a manner that renews us physically, emotionally, mentally, spiritually, and socially.

Healing: observing the day in such a way as to foster healing, relief, release, liberation, and refreshment. Any action that hurts oneself or others is Sabbathbreaking.

Celebrating the creation, or birthday, of the world, and of our redemption. Its atmosphere should be one of celebration, joy, and delight.

Sanctifying: keeping the Sabbath day holy; setting it apart for a special focus on God, His Word, and His agenda, to seek intimacy with Him, embrace Him wholly, and nurture a love relationship with Him that makes us holy.

Remembering, reflecting, and rejoicing about creation, redemption, and Christ's second coming and the creation of the new earth.

Worshipping: participating in corporate, focused worship of God with our church family.

Basking: enjoying, studying, experiencing, and basking in the world God made, rather than working at maintaining it.

Responding: a joyful human response to God's grace in obedience to His loving command to remember Him and His Sabbath gift.

Trusting God to take care of what we leave undone during the hours of the Sabbath. Learning to depend on God rather than on ourselves.

Fellowshipping: nurturing our relationships with family and friends.

Affirming: rightly representing the atmosphere of the Sabbath by a spirit of acceptance, love, and affirmation rather than a spirit of judgment and criticism.

Serving other people in love and witnessing lovingly for God.

Caring for necessary physical needs on Sabbath; no creature—animal or human—should be allowed to suffer on this day.[6]

These biblical principles will always reflect God, His nature, and His character. When we prayerfully focus on them, the Holy Spirit can guide us in their appropriate application to Sabbath keeping within our diverse cultures and life circumstances.

Take a breather—what God really wants
Isaiah 58 is a prophetic manifesto highlighting authentic dedication and commitment against formal religion. In a world marked by injustice and oppression, Isaiah calls us to the real—not the artificial. These include the way we fast and the way we keep the Sabbath. The following texts represent highlights from this crucial chapter.

> *"Is this not the fast that I have chosen:*
> *To loose the bonds of wickedness,*
> *To undo the heavy burdens,*
> *To let the oppressed go free,*
> *And that you break every yoke?*
> *Is it not to share your bread with the hungry,*
> *And that you bring to your house the poor who are cast out;*
> *When you see the naked, that you cover him,*
> *And not hide yourself from your own flesh?" (Isaiah 58:6, 7, NKJV).*

In the face of systemic injustice, we are called to labor for the abolition of every system that diminishes the worth and liberty of the people around us. But we cannot only engage with structures and systems— we must get personally involved, for that is the way of Jesus.

> *"If you turn away your foot from the Sabbath,*
> *From doing your pleasure on My holy day,*
> *And call the Sabbath a delight,*
> *The holy day of the LORD honorable,*
> *And shall honor Him, not doing your own ways,*
> *Nor finding your own pleasure,*
> *Nor speaking your own words,*
> *Then you shall delight yourself in the LORD;*

Sabbath Rest

And I will cause you to ride on the high hills of the earth,
And feed you with the heritage of Jacob your father" (Isaiah 58:13, 14,
NKJV).

The close proximity between the Sabbath and fasting suggests that in Isaiah's time, some thought that this day of celebrating community with the Creator and Redeemer was a day of self-imposed deprivations.

We are blessed with delight when we connect with the Lord of the Sabbath. Isaiah 58 mentions twice the notion of "delight" (verses 13, 14, NKJV). The Hebrew term is not often used in the Old Testament, but poetic texts link delight in the Lord with divine blessings and "the desires of your heart" (Psalm 37:4). Isaiah 58:13 contrasts human pleasure to God-centered delight. Instead of pursuing the siren-breathed whisperings of selfishness, God invites us to experience the sheer delight of discovering His sustaining and creative grace as we serve society's downtrodden.

1. Sonja Steptoe, "Ready, Set, Relax!" *Time*, October 22, 2003, http://content.time.com/time/magazine/article/0,9171,524490-1,00.html.

2. Maria Newman, "Ridgewood Embraces Family Night," *New York Times*, March 27, 2003, https://www.nytimes.com/2003/03/27/nyregion/ridgewood-embraces-family-night.html.

3. A. J. Swoboda, *Subversive Sabbath: The Surprising Power of Rest in a Nonstop World* (Grand Rapids, MI: Brazos, 2018), 12; emphasis in the original.

4. Mathilde Frey, "The Sabbath in the Pentateuch: An Exegetical and Theological Study" (PhD diss., Andrews University, 2011), 282.

5. Sigve K. Tonstad, *The Lost Meaning of the Seventh Day* (Berrien Springs, MI: Andrews University Press, 2009), 479.

6. May-Ellen Colón, "Making Sabbath a 'Happy Day,'" *Adventist Review*, July 1, 2016, https://www.adventistreview.org/1607-35.

CHAPTER
Eleven

Longing for More

A visit to the Israel Museum in Jerusalem is well worth it. The museum has many fascinating ancient artifacts on display, and visitors from all over the world come to enjoy the exhibits. Strangely enough, one of the most popular displays is a fairly modern large model of ancient Jerusalem. The 2,000-square-meter (21,520-square-foot) outdoor model depicts Jerusalem in the second temple period. It was built to a 1:50 scale, which means that a person would be about 35 mm (1.37 inches) tall. Hans Kroch began the building on the grounds of his hotel. In 2006, the model was brought to the Israel Museum in a thousand pieces and reassembled with the help of historians and archaeologists in order to make the model as accurate as possible. Great attention has been paid to detail. The gold-trimmed second temple, with its large courtyard, first draws visitors' attention. Herod's palace can be identified easily. Visitors slowly walk around the perimeter of the model while listening to a guide explain the various buildings.[1]

Why do visitors like looking at a model of the city of Jerusalem when they are *in* the actual city of Jerusalem? Walking around the second temple model is a wonderful visual aid, which helps visitors get a better perspective of Jerusalem's archaeological sites. While no one will mistake this model for the real thing, it helps illustrate ancient realities that are hard to visualize. The Bible, too, is full of miniature models of activities and institutions that all point to larger heavenly realities.

Issue—understanding patterns

Patterns abound all around us. We see them in nature. (Have you ever wondered about the pattern of sand dunes?) We hear patterns in music. We can watch them in sports. Patterns can also be found in Scripture. The study of types (called typology) is based on the fact that there is a pattern in God's work throughout salvation history. "God prefigured His redemptive work in the OT and fulfilled it in the NT," writes New Testament scholar Tom Shepherd.[2]

"The English word 'type' comes from the Greek noun *tupos*," which can mean " 'form,' . . . 'pattern,' 'graven image,' 'outline/sketch,' and 'rough draft.' "[3] It is important to remember that typology should not be confused with allegory. "Allegory is imaginative; it does not reflect the historical sense of the text but treats it with unbridled freedom. Typology, on the contrary, is based on historical connections and is bound to the historical sense of Scripture."[4] The allegorical method of interpretation was used extensively during the Middle Ages, resulting in fanciful interpretations. Sometimes modern preachers are guilty of allegorization and give credence to this method that imposes meaning upon the text of the Bible. "The three gifts of the magi—gold, frank-incense, and myrrh—are allegorized into justification, sanctification, and glorification. The four anchors cast out from the boat that Paul was in on his way to Rome (Acts 27:29) are allegorized as salvation, the church, the home, and the family."[5] Clearly, there are no hints whatsoever in the biblical texts that the authors wanted to communicate these meanings.

Typology, on the other hand, takes its clues from the biblical text itself. First Corinthians 10:1–13 reviews the Exodus experience of biblical Israel and applies it to spiritual Israel. "All our fathers were under the cloud, all passed through the sea, all were baptized into Moses in the cloud and in the sea, all ate the same spiritual food, and all drank the same spiritual drink" (verses 1–4, NKJV), writes Paul, referring to real history. He then connects this history to Jesus, the "spiritual Rock" (verse 4), affirming the fact that Jesus, the God-man, was also instrumental and at work in Israel's past—as He is in the present. Verses 6 and 11 use the Greek word *tupos*, translated in the New King James Version as "examples."

Typology helps us discern the deeper meaning of a biblical text as we are guided by the text itself. For example, the Passover lamb is a type of Christ (see 1 Corinthians 5:7). The bronze serpent raised on the pole in the wilderness is also a type of the crucified Christ (John 3:14). These connections are already implicit in the original context of a given Old Testament text. They are not an afterthought or the result of creative and inventive thinking. God uses patterns to help us understand complex issues.

Worldview—living in expectation
The biblical writers all seemed to have a sense of urgency. Old Testament authors wrote of the "day of the Lord." Peter, Paul, James, and other New Testament authors believed and taught that Jesus was coming soon. This event would not be low-key but be the greatest event in history. "The heavens will disappear with a roar; the elements will be destroyed by fire, and the earth and everything done in it will be laid bare" (2 Peter 3:10).

How do we live as we wait for His imminent return? The soon coming of Jesus has been the great "precursor for change and was the driving force for the rapid spread of the gospel throughout most of the Roman Empire within"[6] the first generation of Christianity. It was also this belief that helped fire the Reformation and birthed the founding of the Advent movement. Although the soon coming of Jesus has already impacted the course of history, believers are not so heavenly minded that they are of no earthly good. Immediately following the momentous signs of the end of the world given in Matthew 24, Jesus goes on to tell three stories about how to live as we watch for the signs of His coming. He tells the story of the ten virgins, emphasizing being prepared for the long wait and living patiently in a ready state by constantly having a supply of the oil of the Holy Spirit (Matthew 25:1–13).

Then Jesus tells the story of the man who goes on a long journey and leaves his servants with a number of talents. The parable suggests that, while living in anticipation of His coming, we are called to use and improve every ability that we have been given to the glory of the Master (verses 14–30). Living in expectation will be living life to the full.

Jesus' third parable describes the final judgment and uses the imagery of a shepherd separating sheep from goats. Here Jesus points out that the ordinary, everyday work, challenges, and opportunities we are confronted with are, in reality, anything but ordinary. It is here, just living normal life, that our belief in the soon coming of Jesus really shows itself in the acts of service that we do for those around us (verses 31–46). As we eagerly wait and serve, we bring heaven a little closer, and when that final event occurs, there will be no frantic surprises, for we have been living in anticipation of history's greatest event all our lives.

Digging deep—behold! the Lamb

Communication is all about connecting, and people living in the twenty-first century connect in abundant ways: Tweets, constantly updated social media feeds, text alerts, news breaks, overflowing email inboxes, and incessant TikTok loops. We thrive on communication, but that does not mean that we always understand what we see, hear, or read.

Context is crucial, for it helps us make sense of realities that are often complex. Context is also crucial when we read Scripture. Most of us understand stories and narratives intuitively. It does not matter whether we live in southern Africa or downtown New York. A good story grabs us, engages us, often moves us, and sometimes even challenges us to action. That is why narrative is one of the most common genres found in the Bible.

Other genres, however, are more complex. When did you last spend significant time in the chapters describing the rituals and offerings associated with Israel's sanctuary cult, which are found in large swaths of Exodus, Leviticus, and Numbers? We may read these texts as part of a yearly Bible-reading plan, but we often sigh with relief once we have reached Deuteronomy or Joshua. Most people who are living in the twenty-first century in a Western context struggle when they come across ritual texts. These texts feel strange and far removed from our reality; they are often bloody and extremely detailed. In fact, ask any Christian about these texts and the complex instructions associated with sacrifices, offerings, washings, and libations, and many will mutter "righteousness by works" under their breath. Let us look a bit closer at some of these texts.

The book of Leviticus contains most of the prescriptions about offerings and sacrifices.[7] Some offerings included libations involving oil or wine that were poured out before God (e.g., Exodus 29:40; Leviticus 23:13) or grain offerings involving flour (e.g., Leviticus 2:1, 2, 4, 5; 23:13). Distinct offering types addressed distinct situations. Peace offerings (or *shelamim*), also translated as "fellowship" or "well-being" offerings (Leviticus 7:11–21; etc.), were offered to praise God (e.g., verse 12; 1 Samuel 11:15), not to attain atonement or forgiveness for a particular sin. The burnt offering (or *'olah*) was burned on the altar (Leviticus 7:8) and often appeared in contexts of national crisis (e.g., 1 Samuel 7:9; 1 Kings 18:38) or celebration (e.g., 1 Kings 9:25). The daily burnt offerings (*tamid*), offered in the morning and in the evening on behalf of the entire people, pointed to Israel's constant dependence on God's forgiving grace (Exodus 29:38–46). Sin offerings (*khatta't*), also translated as "purification offerings," were required once people recognized an unintentional sin (Leviticus 4:22,

23, 27, 28). They were also used in cases of material impurities, such as when a person had recovered from a skin disease (Leviticus 14:19). They illustrated the fact that sin required purification from moral faults, even though some offerings (such as the case of material impurities mentioned above) were not considered "sins" but represented aspects of the life cycle of mortality that resulted from sin.

Once we start to engage with the details of ritual texts involving sacrifices and offerings, we recognize even more profoundly the destructive and contagious nature of sin that required a drastic response. The life of an innocent animal was offered to remove the sin that had symbolically been transferred from the sinner to the sacrificial animal. Through the sprinkling of blood, these sins "accumulated" in the sanctuary during the year. The Day of Atonement (Leviticus 16) offered a visual illustration of the way God would ultimately achieve *at-one-ment*.

The New Testament authors also understood the seriousness of sin. When John the Baptist saw Jesus coming toward him, he exclaimed, "Behold! The Lamb of God who takes away the sin of the world!" (John 1:29, NKJV). The sin offering, as well as other sacrifices, prefigured the sacrificial death of Christ, who offered Himself as a sin offering for humanity's sin (see Romans 8:3). As noted in the commentary on Leviticus in the *Andrews Bible Commentary*: "He [Jesus] took upon Himself our sins and voluntarily and vicariously accepted responsibility for them, dying in our place (2 Cor. 5:21). . . . Through Christ, God provided the sin offering that cleanses all who seek Him (Rom. 3:25; Eph. 5:2). This is the ultimate sacrifice that cleanses humanity once and for all."[8]

Patterns and models are designed to help us understand the big picture. The sacrifices and offerings were never meant as a solution to the sin problem affecting individuals and God's entire creation. Rather, they pointed to God's ultimate answer to sin—the God-man who offered Himself as a sacrifice to take away the sin of the world.

Implications—going home

The Epistle to the Hebrews offers another glimpse of the relationship between type and antitype. Hebrews 3 compares Jesus Christ to Moses and suggests that Israel's experience in the wilderness could function as a paradigm for Christians waiting for the return of Jesus Christ. The author of Hebrews quotes extensively from Psalm 95:7–11 and concludes with God's oath: "So I swore in My wrath, 'They shall not enter My rest' " (Hebrews 3:11, NKJV). In the context of the Old Testament wilderness narrative, this rest referred to Israel's arrival and conquest of the Promised Land. In Hebrews, the context suggests something bigger because the wilderness generation had failed (verses 16–19).

The next chapter repeats the same quote (Hebrews 4:3) and exhorts readers to remember God's promise of entering His rest. (If Hebrews 4 were a movie, there would be a cut between verses 3 and 4.) God's Sabbath rest is somehow related to the rest found when entering the Promised Land. Listen to the final verses of this section: "For if Joshua had given them rest, then He [God] would not afterward have spoken of another day. There remains therefore a rest for the people of God. For he who has entered His rest has himself also ceased from his works as God did from His" (verses 8–10, NKJV). We joyously anticipate this rest from our own attempts to save ourselves, from the pain and sufferings of this world, and from our restlessness.

Take a breather—He is more excellent

Jesus is the true Giver of rest. The author of Hebrews exalts Him again and again, for Jesus is the real deal.

"Jesus has been found worthy of greater honor than Moses, just as the builder of a house has greater honor than the house itself. For every house is built by someone, but God is the builder of everything. 'Moses was faithful as a servant in all God's house,' bearing witness to what would be spoken by God in the future. But Christ is faithful as the Son over God's house. And we are his house, if indeed we hold firmly to our confidence and the hope in which we glory" (Hebrews 3:3–6). While Moses

was surely God's appointed leader during the time of the Exodus, he, too, needed a Savior. He needed grace. Jesus is ever faithful and is the cornerstone of the living temple—His church (Ephesians 2:20).

"Therefore, my friends, since we have confidence to enter the sanctuary by the blood of Jesus, by the new and living way that he opened for us through the curtain (that is, through his flesh), and since we have a great priest over the house of God, let us approach with a true heart in full assurance of faith, with our hearts sprinkled clean from an evil conscience and our bodies washed with pure water. Let us hold fast to the confession of our hope without wavering, for he who has promised is faithful" (Hebrews 10:19–23, NRSV). We can be confident and bold as we enter the sanctuary where forgiveness is offered by the blood of Jesus—no hesitation, no worry, and no fear—for He is our Great High Priest. When we understand the pattern of God's plan of salvation, we can live full of assurance, without wavering.

---

1. For more information, see "Holyland Model of Jerusalem," Madain Project, accessed November 18, 2020, https://madainproject.com/holyland_model_of_jerusalem.

2. Tom Shepherd, "Interpretation of Biblical Types, Allegories, and Parables," in *Understanding Scripture: An Adventist Approach*, ed. George W. Reid (Silver Spring, MD: Biblical Research Institute, 2006), 223.

3. Shepherd, 224.

4. Gerhard Hasel, *Understanding the Living Word of God*, Adventist Library of Christian Thought, vol. 1 (Mountain View, CA: Pacific Press®, 1980), 214.

5. Shepherd, "Interpretation of Biblical Types," 228.

6. " 'Your Sons and Daughters Will Prophesy': The Gift of Prophecy and the Second Coming," *Adventist Review*, October 13, 2015, https://www.adventistreview.org/1525-12.

7. The following is based on Gerald A. Klingbeil, "Sacrifice and Offerings," in *The Oxford Encyclopedia of the Bible and Theology*, ed. Samuel E. Balentine (New York: Oxford University Press, 2015), 251–259.

8. *Andrews Bible Commentary*, ed. Ángel Manuel Rodríguez, Daniel Kwame Bediako, Carl P. Cosaert, and Gerald A. Klingbeil (Berrien Springs, MI: Andrew University Press, 2020), 249.

Twelve

The Ultimate Rest

Yo-Yo Ma is a world-famous cello player. He has stayed in hundreds, perhaps thousands, of hotel rooms during his five-decade-long music career. So there was nothing immediately unusual about his visit to New York City's Peninsula Hotel on October 16, 1999.

Nothing unusual, that is, until the taxi Ma had taken to the hotel after an appearance at Carnegie Hall pulled away—with his irreplaceable $2.5 million cello, built by Domenico Montagnana in 1733, in the taxi's trunk.

"I did something really stupid. . . . I just forgot," Ma sheepishly explained the next day to news reporters. A priceless object lost! There are remarkable stories of dogs, cats, and other pets finding their way home, but this cello had no way of getting back home on its own.

Fortunately, the Peninsula Hotel's staff immediately sprang into action to help Yo-Yo Ma recover his cello. Hundreds of phone calls went out to every taxi company in town. First, the company and then the individual taxi had to be identified, tracked down, and contacted. The group effort paid off. The missing cello was returned within hours, safe and sound.[1]

So much for priceless objects; what about human beings? We have no way of finding our way back to Eden lost. The only sure thing we see is the finality of death. How do we wait expectantly for the ultimate rest of heaven when the waiting seems endless?

Issue—the complicated wait
No one likes waiting, especially for the big things in life, such as the second coming of Jesus. Perhaps this explains why some Christians seem to be particularly vulnerable to conspiracy theories that involve international intrigue by powerful families or religious figures. They quickly latch on to each and every happening as a sure indication that the "time of trouble" (Daniel 12:1, NKJV) is upon us. Some people go so far as to discover strange new ways of deciphering hidden messages in prophecy, which lead to setting dates for end-time events. It seems as if conspiracy theories are particularly tantalizing because they make us feel special, they help us make sense of a chaotic and complicated world, and they make our present reality seem more exciting.

Knowing something that most others do not know also helps us feel more secure and in control. While we are called to "be wise as serpents" (Matthew 10:16, NKJV), we do not have to understand and know all the inner workings of the devil to combat him successfully. We are encouraged to "trust in the LORD . . . , and lean not on . . . [our] own understanding" (Proverbs 3:5, NKJV). We should never feel the need to get ahead of or beyond what God has shown us in His Word. He will tell us what we need to know in His time, and there are things we do not need to know (Mark 13:32; Deuteronomy 29:29). When we indulge in conspiracy theories, we often become afraid and spread fear. This is the opposite of how we are called to live and work for Christ. "God has not given us a spirit of fear, but of power and of love and of a sound mind" (2 Timothy 1:7, NKJV). While these theories can offer easy answers to complicated issues, indulging in them makes us impatient and critical of those who do not share our views and distracts us from what our life's work and mission should be (cf. 1 Timothy 1:4).

As we wait and live in expectation of the Second Coming, we do not have to be in a continual state of hyped-up excitement. We know that God's promises are true, and with the long history of fulfilled biblical prophecy as faith-affirming evidence, we can wait. We know that God is using this waiting time to draw more of His children into His kingdom. He also wants to use this period of time to build our patience, transform our characters, and teach us total dependence on Him. We can rest in His plan and His timing.

Worldview—ready and rested
Ask anyone about the definition of a prophet, and they will, most likely, tell you that a prophet predicts the future. We seem to think that prophecy has to do entirely with what is to come. In reality, prophecy is a lot more than just a sneak preview of some future event. Prophecy is given to save us from destruction and protect us from deception. Biblical prophecy is framed with God's warning, His advice, and ultimately, His redemptive plan of salvation.

The first prophecy was given to Adam and Eve as they were dismissed from their idyllic garden following sin's entrance (Genesis 3:15). This wide-sweeping Messianic prophecy was given to instill hope in our first parents when all seemed lost. A Redeemer would come and would crush the serpent. Over the course of thousands of years, God sent messages through His prophets to warn and encourage His people. Predictions of destruction, exile, and return always served to build believers' faith. Fulfilled prophecy gives us a track record to base our faith on (cf. John 14:29) so that we can trust the future events that God has promised.

Seventh-day Adventist Christians are part of a prophetic movement, and prophecy helps us define who we are and where we are in the light of history. It shows our beginning, our purpose, and our reason for existence. Prophecy actively involves us in God's plans for reaching the world with the good news of His second coming (Matthew 24:14).

The purpose of prophecy is not that we can use insider knowledge to play the market better or secure our personal physical safety. In showing us the broad strokes of the divine schedule for end-time events, God wants us to be able to rest confidently in His love, even when everything around us is falling apart.

Resting confidently does not just apply to the abrupt upheaval of the Second Coming. Prophecy also helps us live in a state of readiness and dependence on God that keeps us prepared for death, which could come at any moment. As we wait for the glorious culmination of history, we can face the future unafraid, knowing that death is an unconscious sleep (John 11:11–14).

Digging deep—homeward bound

God's plan for humanity in Eden was simple—a perfect place, a perfect climate, perfect relationships, and perfect communion with the Creator. The entrance of sin changed all of this, and death became the most dramatic expression of this change. Since then, suffering, pain, loss, and death have been part of our experience. Yet we can never get used to them. We wonder, we worry, we are afraid, and we shake.

Many people around us are worried about the future and, most of all, death. Followers of Jesus are not exempt from this fear. We, too, pass through dark valleys and experience painful losses. Yet we know that we can cast all of our cares on Him who cared so deeply for us that He died for us on the cross and then rose from the dead (see 1 Peter 5:7). In fact, it is the resurrection hope that helps us overcome our fears about the future and death. Listen to Paul's reasoning in his first letter to the Corinthians: "Now if Christ is preached that He has been raised from the dead, how do some among you say that there is no resurrection of the dead? But if there is no resurrection of the dead, then Christ is not risen. And if Christ is not risen, then our preaching is empty and your faith is also empty" (1 Corinthians 15:12–14, NKJV). Paul's logic makes sense. If the Bible's record is unreliable regarding the resurrection of Jesus, how can we trust it to be true when it talks about the second coming of Christ and the resurrection of all those who have fallen asleep in Him? If, however, the resurrection of Jesus is indeed a historical event, then we can be assured that God's promises about the future are true and faithful—and not just foolish talk.

The early Christian community anxiously waited for the second coming of Christ—as did a myriad of Christians following them. Likewise, Seventh-day Adventist Christians wait for the Second Coming and have even included this hope in the name of their denomination.

Paul's first letter to the church in Thessalonica contains a powerful description of the second coming of Jesus. There were probably many members in this church who had lost loved ones, and they were all waiting for Jesus to return. "But I do not want you to be ignorant, brethren, concerning those who have fallen asleep, lest you sorrow as others who have no hope. For if we believe that Jesus died and rose again, even so God will bring with Him those who sleep in Jesus" (1 Thessalonians 4:13, 14, NKJV).

Paul reminds his audience that there is clarity in Jesus' teaching and in Scripture about this most important event in history. Death is aptly described as an unconscious sleep. Dead people have no worries. They rest in their graves. But for those who died trusting in Jesus, death is not the final destination. Paul continues,

> For this we say to you by the word of the Lord, that we who are alive and remain until the coming of the Lord will by no means precede those who are asleep. For the Lord Himself will descend from heaven with a shout, with the voice of an archangel, and with the trumpet of God. And the dead in Christ will rise first. Then we who are alive and remain shall be caught up together with them in the clouds to meet the Lord in the air. And thus we shall always be with the Lord. Therefore comfort one another with these words (verses 15–18, NKJV).

The dead in Christ will be resurrected, and together with those who are alive, they will rise to meet the Lord of the universe in the air. It sounds like science fiction or a Marvel comic book, but it is so much better. As Paul said, "We shall always be with the Lord" (verse 17, NKJV). This is the one place in the universe where we truly will be able to rest in Him. We can embrace Him, thank Him, and just sit quietly with Him—always. We cannot explain eternity, but we can imagine being with our best Friend forever. No more death, no more goodbyes, and no more ventilators and intensive care units.

Paul concludes this important section with the exhortation to "comfort one another with these words" (verse 18, NKJV). Knowing that they would see their loved ones again must have been encouraging to those who were anxiously waiting for the return of Jesus. We, too, are encouraged to comfort one another with these words of hope. Death is not the end. The grave is not the final resting place for those who love Jesus. Hope is baked into Christianity—this blessed hope is central to what we believe. It points us to the rest that God offers those who trust Him, no matter what comes their way.

Implications—our "magnetic" map

Some time ago, we saw our first large sea turtle while snorkeling in the Philippines. It was a majestic sight. Effortlessly, yet purposefully, this beautiful creature swam past us. We tried to follow it for a while, but it swam too fast.

Sea turtles are particular when it comes to reproduction. Researchers have found that large loggerhead turtles who have hatched on beaches in Florida or North Carolina will take eight thousand–mile migratory journeys around the North Atlantic basin. Only one turtle in four thousand survives the immense dangers of this journey, but when they return between six to twelve years later, they return to the exact same beach to lay their eggs and start the cycle again.

How do loggerhead turtles know which is the correct beach? How do they find their way home? Researchers have found that loggerhead turtles are born with an inherited "magnetic map," which guides them back to their beginnings.[2]

Similarly, God has created each of us with a "magnetic map" to heaven. He has put a sliver of eternity into our hearts. There is a hole in our soul that we cannot fill with objects, people, property, or trust funds. When we allow God to find us, that hole is filled by His Spirit, and we begin our journey home. Suddenly, there is a purpose in our hearts that goes beyond *I* and *me, me, me*. Jesus becomes the guiding force in our life, leading us into eternity.

Like the magnetic map of the loggerhead turtle, we, too, have to travel through treacherous waters and experience dangerous moments. Yet we keep moving forward, even when we cannot see around the corner, because Jesus carries all the things that burden us. He must have had this journey in mind when He said, "Come to me, all you who are weary and burdened, and I will give you rest" (Matthew 11:28).

We follow the map. We trust in His Spirit. We rest in Him, for we are going home.

Take a breather—He is coming
In a world marked by confusion, pain, and ever-present tensions, we need a point of guidance to avoid losing our way. For followers of Jesus, the hope in His second coming is this guide. It causes us to lift up our eyes and focus on the most important things. It also helps us gain perspective on what is happening in our lives and those around us.

"Let your gentleness be evident to all. The Lord is near" (Philippians 4:5). Paul lived in the expectation of the soon return of Jesus. This practical exhortation is part of a bigger section describing the characteristics of God's people. Gentleness; joy (cf. verse 4); peace; and, above all, an attitude of prayer are Paul's suggestions as we live in expectation.

"For the grace of God has appeared that offers salvation to all people. It teaches us to say 'No' to ungodliness and worldly passions, and to live self-controlled, upright and godly lives in this present age, while we wait for the blessed hope—the appearing of the glory of our great God and

Savior, Jesus Christ" (Titus 2:11–13). Paul's letter to Titus is full of practical advice to a trusted coworker and church planter. In Jesus, we can clearly see God's grace, offering salvation to all people. This, in turn, moves us to reject ungodliness and sinful passions that separate us from our Redeemer and instead live self-controlled, authentic, and godly lives. While we wait, work, and sometimes wonder, we expect the blessed hope. He will not return to a humble manger but will appear in glory and majesty as the King of kings and Lord of lords.

---

1. Beth Gardiner, "Yo-Yo Ma's Cello Returned," CBS News, October 17, 1999, https://www.cbsnews.com/news/yo-yo-mas-cello-returned/.

2. Lily Whiteman, "Loggerhead Turtle Migration Follows Magnetic Map," *LiveScience*, June 20, 2012, https://www.livescience.com/21080-loggerhead-turtle-migration.html.

Thirteen

Rested Enough— Ready to Go?

Camping was only for the hardy. A space had to be cleared and leveled. Rocks and debris were removed before the heavy wooden tent poles could be put up to support the canvas tent. Heavy guylines pegged the tent to the ground, and a trench was dug around it to keep the rain from washing inside. Campers slept on blankets or sleeping bags on the ground. Food was cooked over an open fire, and bathing had to be done in a nearby pond or river. Camping was fun, but no one mistook it for home. Gradually, the experience became more comfortable with better tents and blow-up mattresses. Soon motor homes arrived, with almost every convenience that one enjoys at home. Today, for a hefty price, one can go glamping.

Glamping is a form of luxury camping started by wealthy people who wanted the experience of African safaris without any of the potential inconveniences. Instead of roughing it in the wilderness, people paid to have luxury accommodations with soft beds and fluffy pillows while enjoying African wildlife.

Today glamping has become even more exotically comfortable. One does not have to walk or hike to a remote wilderness campsite. A private helicopter will take a client to a state-of-the-art luxury accommodation at a secluded spot where the camper can enjoy being served by a personal chef and butler. If that does not sound exciting enough, there is the option of a private concert in a dormant volcano. These are supposed to be relaxing, restful vacations. With this much luxury, one would probably never want to leave and go back to real life.[1]

Getting too comfortable can be a spiritual problem too. There is a big, restless world out there, far away but also close by, right where we are. That world needs to hear about the God who loves us unconditionally—the God who offers forgiveness, grace, and true rest. How are the people of this world to hear if no one tells them?

Issue—differences that divide and unite
There are so many forces that make us who we are. We are all born into a certain culture, speaking a particular language. We live within the confines of a given political, socioeconomic reality. We belong to different tribes and racial groups. None of these distinguishing features are good or bad in themselves, although they are not value free. Each facet of our makeup intimately links us to certain systems of beliefs and attitudes about ourselves and others.

Unfortunately, we have all absorbed deep-seated prejudices. We can see these at play in every country and culture on Earth. In some places, legislation is designed to keep one particular group from enjoying the rights and privileges that other groups have. Although openly admitting to prejudices is discouraged in most places, horrific genocides and hate crimes keep showing how deeply rooted prejudice is in humanity. Unfortunately, deep-seated prejudices do not disappear when we become Christians. Although we may recognize, at least on a cognitive level, that God loves everyone, we often have trouble realizing and demonstrating the breadth of this love.

God does not want anyone to be lost; He desires "everyone to come to repentance" (2 Peter 3:9). "Everyone" includes people from other tribes and races. "Everyone" includes non-Christians and people of other denominations. "Everyone" even includes murderers, terrorists, child molesters, and the most disgusting people we can think of. God's grace is not exclusive, which only very few can rest in. God loves all people (John 3:16). All people need salvation, and God chooses us to be the ones to invite them to Christ. Only as we leave our comfort zones and mix with people who are different from us do we begin to discover our own deep-seated prejudices, which we had no idea we even had. As we turn these prejudices over to God and ask for healing, we get to reexperience God's grace, and we find a true and wonderful family in people who are different from us. Only when we are enveloped in God's grace can we, collectively, find rest.

Worldview—us versus them
We live in an increasingly polarized world. We talk about liberals versus conservatives, young versus old, rich versus poor, environmentalists versus those who consider climate change to be a hoax, urban dwellers versus those living in rural areas, and black versus white. We could continue this list for a long time. Polarization does not stop at the door of our churches. We argue with those we consider "too conservative," "too liberal," "too focused on social engagement," or "too health conscious." Often, we think in terms of *us* versus *them*. New Testament scholar Oleg Kostyuk writes,

> "Us" is usually a group of people who have similar social, cultural, and ethnic backgrounds and share interests, as well as political and religious views. "Us" is a group of people with whom we feel comfortable.
>
> "They" look different, think different, and speak different. Most of the time we limit our interactions with "them."[2]

Racism is one of the expressions of *us* versus *them* that we are familiar with. Racism is as old as this planet, for there were always those who thought that they were markedly different from others, and different, in most cases, meant that they were "better" and others were inherently inferior.

Jonah thought of the Ninevites as "them." The Assyrians were a cruel bunch. Historical and archaeological records confirm Jonah's misgivings. The Assyrians were brutal and merciless when they dealt with rebellion and uprisings. They were particularly sensitive to revolts in Israel and Judah, which were buffer territories separating their empire from Egypt. Numerous historical documents and stone reliefs discovered in the palaces of Assyrian kings offer great insights into Assyrian military practices. "Assyria's military machine was a key factor in the rise of the empire. . . . The custom in the Assyrian army was to conduct campaigns once a year, which the king often led. Each campaign went to a different region, with the purpose of conquering new lands or strengthening the rule of Assyria in that area. As the empire grew, soldiers were drafted into the army from the conquered peoples and stationed in units of their own. The Assyrian soldiers had great stamina and physical abilities and were known for their courage, determination, and ruthlessness."[3]

Jonah had good reason to hate the Assyrians, yet that is not what God wanted him to do. God wanted him to move from an *us*-versus-*them* viewpoint and recognize God's image and likeness even in an Assyrian, for God's value system is completely distinct from the one that drives the *us*-versus-*them* mindset.

Digging deep—getting angry with God
We often wonder why God was so intent on using Jonah as His missionary to Nineveh. There may have been others who would have gladly accepted God's call to preach His judgment message to the large city. God, however, calls Jonah, who quickly recognizes the implications of His call and runs in the opposite direction—away from the presence of the Lord (Jonah 1:3).

While God's miraculous stilling of the storm and His sending a great fish to save Jonah from certain death are excellent material for children's books' illustrations, they do not represent the topical and theological center of the book of Jonah. Nor does the incredible success of Jonah's evangelistic thrust represent the core of Jonah's story. It seems, instead, that the last chapter of the book is the place that requires closer attention and deeper reflection, for it deals with Jonah's image of God and his perception of the character of God, which, by all accounts, lie right at the center of the great controversy raging in this universe.

Jonah 4 begins with an angry prayer by the prophet. Somehow there is a mental disconnect between anger and prayer. "Ah, LORD, was not this what I said when I was still in my country? Therefore I fled previously to Tarshish; for I know that You are a gracious and merciful God, slow to anger and abundant in lovingkindness, One who relents from doing harm. Therefore now, O LORD, please take my life from me, for it is better for me to die than to live!" (verses 2, 3, NKJV).

Jonah has a theological problem. He does not like God's abundant grace, especially when it is directed toward his enemies. He appreciates this grace when it touches his life (e.g., his prayer in Jonah 2:2–9), but there is no hint of grace in this missionary's preaching to the Ninevites (Jonah 3:4). Jonah thinks that God's grace is for "us" (God's chosen people) but not for "them" (cruel Nineveh).

Jonah knows the Torah, the Law. In his prayer, he quotes from Exodus 34:6, 7—one of the key texts describing God's self-revelation in the Old Testament. He "knows" God's character, but he does not like the grace side of God's character. That is why he is ready to die for a second time (after he had earlier told the sailors to throw him into the sea to certain death in Jonah 1:12).

God's answer to Jonah's angry prayer is gentle, didactic, and thought provoking: "Is it right for you to be angry?" (Jonah 4:4, NKJV). There are no accusations, no thunderclaps or lightning strikes, just a simple question, followed by another miraculous sign that illustrates God's character.

God makes a shady plant grow large at lightning speed. Jonah is very pleased (verse 6). He has a front-row seat overlooking Nineveh. He is enjoying the shade, and perhaps, he may even be able to see

God's judgment enacted. Who knows, somebody may mess up in this messed-up city, causing God to send some fire and brimstone.

Nothing of this nature happens. Instead, the shady plant withers and dies, and Jonah sits again under the hot sun. Again, he is angry and wishes to die (verse 8), and again, God responds to his rash death wish with a gentle question. "Is it right for you to be angry about the plant?" (verse 9).

Why does God bother with this runaway prophet who obviously does not want the job? Why is God so insistent on choosing Jonah? Why doesn't God give Jonah a break and let him rest? God knows something that we do not. *Jonah needs the mission trip to Nineveh as much as the Ninevites need to hear the message.*

God calls Jonah to go to Nineveh because Jonah probably has not spent much time thinking about his relationship with the Assyrians before this particular call. He probably knows that he does not like them, but he has no idea *how much* he hates them or the extremes he will go to, to avoid them until he receives God's call. Jonah is definitely not ready to have a Ninevite as a next-door neighbor in heaven. Jonah has not learned to love as God loves.

Implications—not simply *what* but also *why*
The gospel must reach deep—deeper than intellectual consent or rational agreement, deeper than our words, and deeper than even our actions and behavior. The gospel must go right to our motivations in order to achieve the transformation that God has in mind for each one of us. This is especially true when we think of missions.

Jesus put missions on our hearts. He told us to "go therefore and make disciples of all the nations" (Matthew 28:19, NKJV). We sometimes think that simply getting doctrinal information out to people is what witnessing is all about. We think of this as being an "outside" job that needs to be done quickly and efficiently because "this gospel of the kingdom will be preached in all the world as a witness to all the nations, and then the end will come" (Matthew 24:14, NKJV). We may be tempted to think that this simply involves a list of Bible texts that prove the Sabbath, the state of the dead, the literal second coming of Jesus, and other distinctive truths that need to be written on pamphlets and slipped under doors. We may think that mailing a book to every home in a town or zip code will have that area covered. For braver people, this may be taken as a directive to preach a sermon about the Sabbath being the seventh day while on the local metro train. The timider among us may try to get around this directive by supporting the mission activities of others through their generous financial contributions.

While God can and does use these methods to reach others, He really wants mission to be a deeper and more transforming process for the people to be reached and for us. Doing mission outreach with an attitude of "here's the truth—take it or leave it" is anything but rest-ful. Mission is a two-way street. It is a partnership with God; one in which we are invited to yoke together with Him and trust that we will find the true rest He promises (Matthew 11:28). That partnership begins by asking God to give us His passion for people. With that passion, mission becomes not an activity but a way of life. We will not be troubled by the anxious thought, *Have I done enough?* Instead, our outreach activities will expand in a million new and creative ways, driven by a deep love. We will study, pray, and come close to the people God puts on our hearts. We will try to tailor the gospel to reach each of these people, giving them the best opportunity to know the God who loves them unconditionally—the God who offers forgiveness, grace, and true rest.

Take a breather—part of the family business

Jesus' coming to Earth to save humanity and offer atonement to those who are willing to accept His grace is the best expression of *missio Dei*, "God's mission." God invites us to join Him in His mission.

"How, then, can they call on the one they have not believed in? And how can they believe in the one of whom they have not heard? And how

can they hear without someone preaching to them? And how can anyone preach unless they are sent? As it is written: 'How beautiful are the feet of those who bring good news!' " (Romans 10:14, 15). Believing requires that we first hear the good news. In this passage, Paul is quoting a portion of Isaiah 52:7, which is a text given in the context of the victorious God coming home to Jerusalem and bringing salvation.

"But the Lord said to Ananias, 'Go! This man is my chosen instrument to proclaim my name to the Gentiles and their kings and to the people of Israel' " (Acts 9:15). God speaks directly to Ananias, a Christian living in Damascus, to reach out and bless Saul and pray for him. God's call to us can mean reaching out to those who have hurt us, extending His grace to them.

------

1. A number of extravagant glamping experiences have been listed in Tom Marchant, "#The-LIST: The World's Most Extravagant Experiences—and Why They Are Worth It," *Harper's Bazaar*, October 12, 2017, https://www.harpersbazaar.com/culture/travel-dining/g12817107/worlds-most-expensive-experiences/.

2. Oleg Kostyuk, "The Welcoming Jesus," *Adventist World*, June 1, 2020, https://www.adventistworld.org/the-welcoming-jesus/.

3. David Ussishkin, *Biblical Lachish: A Tale of Construction, Destruction, Excavation and Restoration* (Jerusalem: Israel Exploration Society/Biblical Archaeological Society, 2014), 267, 268.

Epilogue

A Prayer for Rest

In a restless world of continual activity, please teach us to stop and recognize our need for rest. We realize that we have caught the contagious virus of restlessness, and without Your intervention, it will grow and explode into open rebellion against You.

Please help us to understand that although this rest You offer is free, it is never cheap.

Help us to win the great battle with self and learn the challenge of daily surrender.

May Your forgiveness that brings rest never become stale or irrelevant to us. May we keep it fresh and actual by forgiving others.

Teach us how to maintain a healthy lifestyle that will prompt both physical and mental rest. When we are sick or face mental health challenges, please help us to rest in the assurance that You love us for who we are and not just what we can do.

Teach us to move to Your rhythms of rest as we delight in celebrating the Sabbath rest that will remind us of who we are.

May we never reduce Your Sabbath rest to a list of dos and don'ts, but rather teach us how to find holy delight in activities that draw us closer to You, others, and Your creation as we anticipate the day when You will make all things new.

Please bring rest to our complicated, tangled relationships. May we be able to find in each person, regardless of race, gender, or ethnicity, someone who is our equal and equally loved by You.

Show us how to live in anticipation of history's greatest event without resorting to frantic alarmist activities. Teach us how to demonstrate our belief in the soon coming of Jesus by selfless acts of service for those around us, which will invite them to find hope and rest in You.

Please build patience in us, transform our characters, and teach us total dependence on You, resting in Your plan and Your timing. May we live in a state of restful readiness, unafraid to face death whenever it comes.

Thank You for choosing us to go as Your messengers to a big, restless world. Help us to abandon our often-distorted images of You and share the beauty of Your character, Your irresistible grace, and Your unswerving compassion for everything lost.

We ask all of this in the name of the One who is our Rest.

Amen.